Love ya,

# Family Circle Quick & Easy Christmas Crafts

Editorial Director/Arthur Hettich
Special Books Editor/Marie T. Walsh
Creative Director/Joseph Taveroni
Editor/Rosemary Drysdale
Art Director/Pam English
Assistant Editor/Flora Suraci
Illustrations/William J. Meyerriecks
Cover Design/ Peter Davis

And the Editors of Family Circle Magazine
and Family Circle Great Ideas

**X Columbia House**

Published by Columbia House, a Division of CBS Inc.,
51 West 52nd Street, New York, New York 10019

# Contents:

Christmas is just too good to pack into a small part of December and then put away until the next year. We at Family Circle have seen the growing trend among our readers to make the most of the holidays by starting early and turning out the most spectacular handmade gifts for family and friends, ornaments and decorations for the house, and gourmet foods for serving and giving—all from the step-by-step directions in the pages of Family Circle and Family Circle Great Ideas.

Here is our selection from the thousands of crafts our readers and editors agree make Christmas more meaningful. Each has simple-to-follow directions that make preparing for the holidays fun for all your family.

ISBN-0-930748-06-9
Library of Congress Catalog Card Number: 78-556-97
Printed in the United States of America
Published by Columbia House, a Division of CBS Inc., 51 West 52nd Street, New York, New York 10019

# Fill the House with Christmas

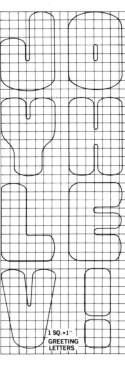

1 SQ.=1"
GREETING
LETTERS

## JOY BANNER

MATERIALS: Fabric scraps (about two 10" square scraps per letter); nylon cording or heavy weight yarn for hangers; polyester stuffing; 3-foot wood dowel, 1" in diameter; two 2½" diameter Styrofoam balls; paint; spray paint intended for use on Styrofoam.

DIRECTIONS for each letter: Following directions on page 140, trace pattern onto paper. Using pattern, cut two fabric pieces. Cut a 9" piece of cording for each letter; fold in half and knot 3" from fold (this forms a loop for hanging). Tack cut ends of cording to top of one fabric piece (tack to right side of fabric at centerpoint of letter). Seam both pieces, right sides together, leaving a 3" opening at top (be careful not to catch cording in seam). Turn right side out. Stuff through opening; slipstitch closed making sure cording extends from top of letter. For exclamation point, join the two pieces with a 2" piece of cording. *To make rod*: Paint dowel. While dowel is drying, use a sharp knife to cut holes in Styrofoam ball to fit dowel ends; spray paint Styrofoam; let dry; glue one Styrofoam ball to end of dowel. Slip letters onto dowel in desired order; slip (do not glue) remaining Styrofoam ball onto other end of dowel; tie a doubled piece of cording to both dowel ends for hanging over door. *Note*: Our pattern offers a total of seven letters, so you can change your greeting to "LOVE" or "HELLO."

*Color photo on page 65*

## NOEL BANNER

Finished size: 13″ × 17½″.

MATERIALS: 17″ × 21½″ piece even-weave linen, 21 threads to the inch; size 20 tapestry needle; 1 spool each #5 pearl cotton for embroidery in the following colors: red, light pink, dark pink, yellow, orange, green, light purple, dark purple; 2 additional spools of any color pearl cotton for tassles and hanger; dressmaker's carbon; shirt cardboard; pencil; scissors; straight pins; transparent tape; tissue paper; embroidery hoop; 14″ × 18½″ piece felt or other fabric for backing; two ½″ diameter dowels, 18″ long; 4 knobs for dowel ends (optional); red spray paint for dowels (optional).

DIRECTIONS: Following directions on page 140, reduce and trace bird design onto tissue paper. Cover both sides of tissue tracing with transparent tape to reinforce; set aside. *To position design*: Borders and letters are all worked in Cross Stitch (*see* BASIC EMBROIDERY STITCHES); each stitch is worked over 3 threads on your fabric with 1-stitch space (also 3 threads) left between worked cross stitches. Using this gauge, make lines of basting stitches to mark off outside border dimensions on linen. (Top and bottom borders are 62 stitches wide, 4 stitches deep. Side borders are 28 stitches down, 4 stitches deep.) Lightly outline letters in basting, counting stitches and spaces in photo on page 65. *To embroider*: Insert linen in embroidery hoop, moving hoop as necessary. Use photo as a guide. Work top and bottom borders, then side borders. Use red and purple for flowers and green for border. Work letters in red. Using tracing of bird, pencil and carbon,

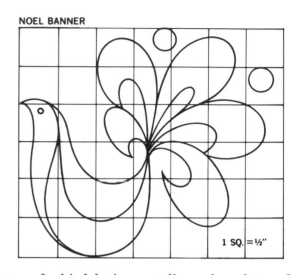

NOEL BANNER

1 SQ. = ½″

transfer bird design onto linen above letter O as shown in photo. Turn tracing over and retrace bird (facing in opposite direction) *under* letter O. Using Chain Stitch (*see* BASIC EMBROIDERY STITCHES), embroider birds. Embroider borders above and below lettering. *To back embroidery*: Lay embroidery wrong side up on a thick towel. Fold side edges over (to wrong side) ¼″ out from embroidered borders; press. Baste, then stitch backing fabric to linen along sides, right sides together. Stitch backing to top edge 2″ above top row of border embroidery; turn right side out. *To make dowel casing*: Turn top under 2″; tack firmly. Finish bottom casing in same way. If you wish, paint dowels and attach decorative knobs. *To make hangers*: Tie 4 long strands of pearl cotton to top dowel ends. *To make tassels*: Wind pearl cotton around 2½″ length of cardboard, 100 times. Slip doubled piece of pearl cotton under strands at top of cardboard; tie off tightly, leaving doubled ends long for tying onto dowel. Cut strands open at bottom; tie strands together ⅓ of the way down from tied off top. Make 4 tassels. Insert dowels into casings; attach tassels to dowel ends.

## YARN-DOLL WREATH

MATERIALS: Purchased wreath. For both dolls: Knitting worsted: *For Balls*: Remnant skeins in colors of your choice. *For girl doll*—One skein (4 oz.) in gold, pink, medium blue and white; 1 skein (3½ oz.) variegated. *For boy doll*—One skein (4 oz.) in dark blue, pink, orange and white; 26 styrofoam balls (varying 1½″, 2″ and 3″ in diameter); white

glue; four black buttons; scrap of red felt; tie wire or beading wire.

DIRECTIONS (are given for girl doll; any changes for boy doll are in parentheses): *Yarn Balls*—Wrap remnant yarn around balls of various sizes until styrofoam is completely covered. Secure yarn-end with a pin. Wire balls to wreath, as shown in photo.

YARN DOLLS

1. *For head, upper body and face*: Cut 80 strands of pink yarn each 30″ long; tie strands together in center. Spread evenly over 3″ ball. Tie strands at bottom of ball, leaving ends free.

2. *For hair*: Cut 78 strands of yellow yarn, each 32″ long; (60 strands orange, each 9″ long) tie strands together in center. Matching centers, attach to head with a fine hairpin. Pull forward about 30 strands and cut to 2″ length for bangs. On each side, tie strands together about 5″ from center "part" down. Below tie, divide strands into three equal parts; braid (do not braid boy's). Tie and trim braid ends, then fasten braid to head with a fine hairpin.

3. *For arms*: Cut 65 strands of pink yarn each 13″ long; tie strands together 1″ from each end.

4. *For sleeves*: Cut 50 strands of white yarn, each 13″ long (60 strands, blue, each 10″ long). Matching centers, lay sleeve strands on arm strands; tie ¾″ from ends of sleeve strands and again 3″ from ends of arms. Place combined strands between pink body yarns divided into two layers. Tie body yarns below arms.

5. *For legs*: Cut 85 strands of pink yarn 12″ long; tie strands together at center and 1″ from each end. Tie legs at center to body yarns.

6. *For Bodice front*: Cut 80 strands of blue (white) yarn 9″ long. Lay the bundle of strands over the front of the head with one end extending ¾″ below the neck. Tie a single yarn around neck to secure the lengths. Flip Bodice yarns down and spread them out across body front. Repeat for Bodice back. About 3½″ below neck, tie a single yarn around doll body, over Bodice yarns, to form waistline.

7. *For skirt (pants) front*: Cut 150 strands of variegated yarn (blue), 14″ (15″) long. Lay the bundle of strands over front with one end extending 7″ below waist. Tie a single yarn around waist and flip upper yarns down. (Divide strands in two; tie at ankles.) Distribute strands evenly across body front with the center of the strands at the waistline.

8. Repeat for skirt (pants) back.

9. *For eyes*: Attach buttons to face with hairpin pushed through the holes.

10. *For mouth:* Glue on a scrap of red felt.

11. Wire dolls to wreath.

## BOXWOOD WREATH

Boxwood wreath has green hedge apples, nandina berries and a big plaid bow.

## FRUIT AND DOVES WREATH

MATERIALS: ½ yard 36″ wide green felt; felt scraps in several colors (we used red, lime, yellow, gold, orange, fuchsia, white and black); Styrofoam wreath frame, 12″ outer diameter and 1¼″ thickness; fabric glue; polyester or cotton stuffing; straight pins.

DIRECTIONS: Cut 1¼″ wide strips from green felt and wind around wreath frame, pinning ends to the back side with straight pins. Following directions on page 140, enlarge patterns shown. Cut out leaves from green felt. Glue on front surface with ends alternately overlapping the inner and outer edge of the wreath. Cut out fruit and doves. Make a line of glue around the edge of each

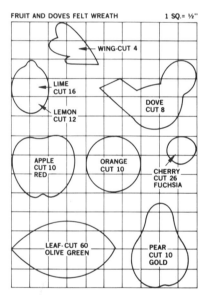

pattern piece and put a bit of stuffing in center. Place stems inside fruit halves (cherry stems on back), and press tops and bottoms together. Let dry. Arrange fruit on wreath and glue down. Make 4 doves, 2 facing in each direction. Use small circles for eyes and pointy shapes for beaks. Cut a small ¼″ strip of white felt; roll up and glue; then glue behind each dove to make it stand out from the wreath. Glue doves in place. From red felt, cut a 30″ strip, 1½″ wide, for the bow. Tie so the streamers are about 7″ long. Attach to wreath with straight pins out of sight between the loops of the bow.

## STUFFED PATCHWORK WREATH

MATERIALS: ½ yd. 36″-wide red or green cotton print fabric; scraps (about 6″ square) of other cotton prints; 3″ square red felt; ⅓ yd. 18″-wide fusible webbing; ⅓ yd. dacron batting; white thread; needle; polyester fiberfill; paper for patterns.

DIRECTIONS: Following directions on page 140, enlarge and trace patterns onto paper. Use pattern to cut 8 wedge shapes of print fabrics, allowing for ¼″ seams all around. Use leaf pattern to cut 8 fabric holly leaves (no seam allowance needed). Cut 8 berries from red felt. Cut matching pieces of webbing for all holly leaf and berry pieces. Pin webbing shapes to wrong sides of fabric shapes. Following manufacturer's directions for webbing, iron one holly leaf and one berry to the center of each fabric wedge. Sew wedge sections together along straight edges, taking ¼″ seams (finished piece will be a circle). Press seams to one side. Using this as a pattern, cut a back for wreath from the ½ yard of fabric; cut a matching circle of batting as well. Pin batting to the wrong side of wreath front; quilt around each leaf and berry with white thread, taking small running stitches. Cut two 2½″-wide strips of fabric (or piece scraps as needed)—one to fit around outside circumference of wreath, and one to fit inside, and be sure to add 2″ to each strip to allow for seam. Right sides together, pin strips to inside and outside edges of wreath top, turning under one short end and overlapping it atop the other where they meet (to form a finished closure). Sew; clip curves. Right sides together, pin wreath back to outside strip; sew. Turn wreath right side out.

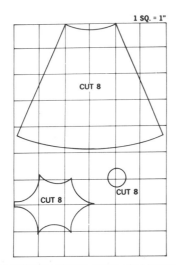

1 SQ. = 1"

CUT 8

CUT 8

CUT 8

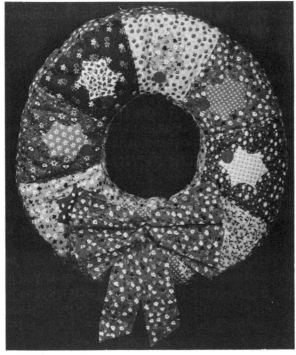

Stuff with fiberfill. Handstitch inner strip to wreath back to close, adding additional stuffing as needed. Fashion a bow from leftover print fabric; stitch to wreath. Hang wreath by simply attaching a safety pin to the back and hanging it on a picture hook.

## CANDY CANE WREATH

MATERIALS: Purchased wreath; 4 dozen 7" candy canes; florist's tape; covered heavy-weight florist's wire; six double bows of weatherproof red "velvet"; hairpins or thread.
DIRECTIONS: Cut wire into 48 lengths, 3½" each. Attach wires to candy canes with floral

tape so that 2" of wire extends beyond bottom. Push wired canes into wreath, and secure bows with hairpins or thread.

## SALT DOUGH ANGEL WREATH
BASIC SALT DOUGH
2 cups all purpose flour*
1 cup salt (iodized)
1 cup water
Combine flour and salt in a large flat-bottomed bowl; mix well with a spoon. Add water, a little at a time, mixing as you pour to form dough into a ball. (*Note*: Additional water may be needed, depending on humidity. Be careful not to add too much, or dough will become sticky.) Knead 7-10 minutes, until dough is smooth, yet firm. Place dough in a plastic bag until ready to use, to prevent drying. Dough may be kept in plastic bag in refrigerator for up to 5 days. *Do not use self-rising flour as it causes sculptures to expand out of shape.
MATERIALS: 1 recipe Basic Salt Dough; heavy-duty aluminum foil; ornament hook or paper clip; straight pin; water color or acrylic paints; spray varnish or shellac.
DIRECTIONS: Tear off a piece of heavy-duty aluminum foil at least 10"×10". Score two circles using the same center, one 1¾" diameter, the other 7¾" diameter. Score lines or "spokes" dividing circles into eight equal

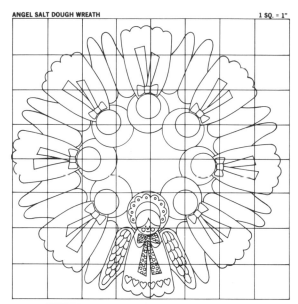

ANGEL SALT DOUGH WREATH                    1 SQ. = 1"

*Color photo on page 65*

parts. These are your guide lines and you will build your wreath on this aluminum foil. Pluck a small piece of dough and roll between your palms into a ball. Flatten and shape to form the body of angel, using the drawing as a guide for size. (Enlarge the drawing, following the directions on page 140.) Body and all other pieces should be about 5/16″ thick. It may require a bit of preliminary practice to get this first piece just right. Remember that no matter what piece you are forming, always begin by rolling the piece of dough between your palms until it is smooth and round, then flatten and shape. Next form a ball of dough and flatten to form halo. Attach it to angel's body by brushing the joining pieces with water. Form head and attach to body on top of halo. Form and add wings. A tiny dot of dough should be added to the head to make a nose. When you are satisfied that your angel is close enough to the guide angel,

you will want to duplicate each piece of the angel eight times so that your wreath will be balanced and equal all the way around. It may be necessary to take this original angel apart in order to match the dough amounts exactly. You should have eight equal chunks of dough apiece for body, halo, head, right and left wings. Put all these pieces in a separate plastic bag so dough doesn't dry out. Place heavy-duty aluminum sheet before you. Using the small and large scored circles as your inner and outer limits, build an angel on each of the eight "spokes" that divide the circles, making sure to wet the joining pieces. Prick each head, halo, body and wing just once with a straight pin so that dough doesn't rise out of shape while baking. Poke in a tiny ornament hook or paper clip at top of wreath for hanging. Bake at 300°F for about 3 hours, or until completely hardened. *Note*: If dough has become quite moist as additional pieces are attached, allow wreath to air dry slightly before placing in the oven, to avoid puffing.) Remove and cool. Paint wreath alternating blue and red angels using photo as a guide. Faces and wings show much of the natural color dough. When painting is finished and dry, spray on clear varnish or shellac. After Christmas, store in a cool place.

## HEART WREATH

GENERAL DIRECTIONS: Following the directions on page 140, enlarge the small (4¼″), medium (5¼″) and large (8″) heart patterns; cut out and label the three widths. Use in the following designs as directed.

1 SQ.=1"

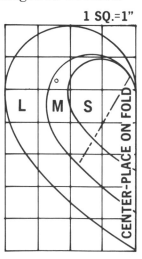

*Color photo on page 65*

## LACE HEARTS

MATERIALS (for twelve each of small and medium hearts): 44"-wide lace fabric, ½ yd.; gold thread; spray starch.

DIRECTIONS:

1. Trace around small and medium heart patterns on lace and cut out one heart for each ornament. Spray hearts with starch to make them stiff.
2. Add gold thread hanger at top of each.

## STUFFED FELT HEARTS

MATERIALS (for seven ornaments): 36"-wide felt, ¼ yd.; 6-strand embroidery floss; synthetic stuffing; gold thread; small embroidery hoop; pinking shears; dressmaker's carbon.

DIRECTIONS:

1. Using medium heart pattern, trace twice (for front and back) on felt for each ornament. *Do not cut out.* On each Front draw a 1¾" diameter circle for wreath.
2. For the *wreath design*, work ten groups of three red French Knots around the circle. Work random green Detached Chain Stitches around each side of the circle to make a wreath about ⅝" wide *(see* BASIC EMBROIDERY STITCHES).
3. Cut out hearts on tracing line using pinking shears. Pin each Front to a Back, right sides out and edges matching. Stitch ¼" from edge, leaving about 2" open for stuffing. Stuff firmly. Stitch opening closed.
4. Thread needle with gold thread. Draw it through the center top of heart and tie ends to form hanger.

## CROSS-STITCH HEART PANELS

MATERIALS (for one large treetop and ten medium hearts): 42"-wide even-weave Perl-Aida cloth, 11-squares-to-the-inch, ¼ yd.; same amount of white felt; red and green 6-strand embroidery floss; gold thread; *for medium hearts*: 5 yds. baby rickrack and 3 yds. 1"-wide grosgrain ribbon; *for large heart*: ¾ yd. regular rickrack, 3 yds. 1"-wide grosgrain ribbon, 1 yd. ¼"-wide grosgrain for ties; white glue.

DIRECTIONS (for medium hanging hearts):

1. Using medium heart pattern trace hearts to Aida cloth, *having center line of pattern on a straight grain of cloth. Do not cut out.* Trace and cut a felt heart for each cloth heart.
2. Following the stitch chart (*see* BASIC EMBROIDERY STITCHES), work Cross Stitch with two strands of floss, centering the design on the heart and covering one square of cloth with each stitch. Press on the wrong side. Cut out the embroidered heart on tracing line.
3. Glue a felt heart to the back of embroidered cloth heart. Starting at the center top, glue rickrack around the edge of the heart.
4. Turn under ½" at top end of 10" piece of ribbon. Cut a notch at the other end. Center heart over ribbon, right sides up, and glue in place.
5. Thread needle with gold thread. Draw it through the ribbon loop and tie ends to form hanger.

### CROSS STITCH CHART

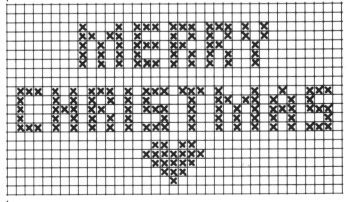

## QUILLED HEARTS

MATERIALS (for about four dozen 5" hearts): Package of 50 paper quilling strips, each

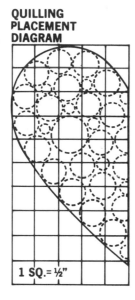

**QUILLING PLACEMENT DIAGRAM**

1 SQ. = ½"

⅛"×20" (we used red and white); quilling tool or large hatpin; gold thread; white glue; wax paper.

DIRECTIONS:

1. Cut paper to length indicated below. Wind paper tightly around the tip of a quilling tool or the sharp end of a large hatpin. It will be easier to start the winding if you dampen your fingers slightly. Roll the paper and the needle between the thumb and forefinger until finished, then slide the coil off the point. Practice until you can maintain even tension.

2. From 8" strip of paper, make 39 coils, ½" in diameter and two coils ¾". From 4" strips make 15 coils ¼" in diameter. Measure across a coil and loosen it if necessary to make it the correct diameter. Place a dot of glue inside the free end and press it to the coil to close.

3. Following directions on page 140, enlarge the heart pattern. The broken lines are for placement and do not need to be traced.

4. Cover heart pattern with wax paper and secure both to a table with masking tape. Starting at outside of heart, place coils in position *(see dotted line)*. Transfer a dot of glue on a toothpick to the sides of the coils where they touch each other. Let them dry.

5. Bring gold thread through a coil at the center top and tie thread ends to make a hanger.

## PATCHWORK HEART

MATERIALS (for seven ornaments): Red and white check gingham for Backs and Front patches; velveteen for patches; 21"-wide iron-on interfacing for Fronts, ¼ yd; ⅜"-wide ribbon, 3½ yds.; ½"-wide lace ruffling, 3½ yds.; gold thread; stuffing.

DIRECTIONS:

1. Using medium heart pattern, cut one heart of interfacing and one heart of Back fabric for each ornament. Using the broken line in the pattern, trace a center patch and a side patch pattern. Cut a pair of gingham side patches and one velveteen center patch for each heart.

2. Pin patches over fusible side of interfacing heart, edges touching. Iron to secure patches. Pin ribbon over touching raw edges and stitch along both edges.

3. Beginning at top center, pin lace to Front, edges matching and finished edge of lace facing inward. Stitch ¼" from edges.

4. Pin Back to Front, over lace, right sides together. Seam over previous stitching, leaving a 2" opening for stuffing. Turn right side out and stuff. Slipstitch opening closed. Tie 8" of ribbon into a small bow and tack it at center top.

5. Thread needle with gold thread. Draw it though the center top of heart and tie ends to form hanger.

## STUFFED SATIN HEART

MATERIALS (for seven ornaments): 44"-wide red satin, ¼ yd.; scraps of green felt; ¼" red wooden beads, 21; gold thread for hanger; stuffing.

DIRECTIONS:

1. Using medium heart pattern, cut a satin Front and Back for each ornament

2. Trace the holly leaf pattern and cut out. Trace twice on green felt for each ornament; cut out.

3. Pin Front to Back, right sides together, edges matching. Stitch ¼" from edges, leaving 2" open for stuffing. Clip curves and turn

**HOLLY LEAF - ACTUAL SIZE**

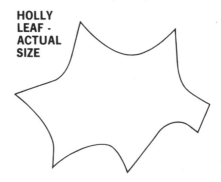

right side out. Stuff and slipstitch opening closed.

4. Lap the leaves a little at top center of heart and sew them in place under three red beads.

5. Thread needle with gold thread. Draw it through the center top of heart and tie ends to form hanger.

## TO DECORATE WREATH

DIRECTIONS: To a store bought wreath attach one medium felt heart, one satin heart, one red quilled heart, one patchwork heart; three small lace hearts and two medium lace hearts. Tie a large bow in the center of the wreath, allowing sufficient ribbon to attach medium cross-stitch heart to center streamer. (See photo). All the extra hearts will make lovely ornaments for your Christmas tree.

## LAWN DECORATIONS

REINDEER SCULPTURES (approximately 5′ tall)—MATERIALS: No. 10 galvanized steel wire (sold in 1-lb. lots) 3 lbs. for one figure; No. 20 wire, 1 lb.; garlands of plastic pine and holly; bee lights; 2″-wide red outdoor ribbon.

DIRECTIONS: The sculptures consist of four series of bent wire sections, constructed over each other, as shown in FIGS. 1 to 5. Use No. 10 wire cut to the following sections.

Cutting:

First: 124″ for first armature.

Second: 124″ for second armature.

Third: 138″ for backbone and rear legs; 108″ for front legs.

Fourth: One 108″ for front legs and one 114″ for rear legs.

Anchor wires: four, 10″ each.

Shape second, third and fourth wires over the first, using No. 20 wire to connect at junctions, as each layer of wire is added. When sculpture is completed, bind all the layers with No. 20 wire.

Affix garlands to sculpture with No. 20 wire. Add holly antlers, lights and ribbon. Bend anchor wires into arch; slip through feet of reindeer and hammer into the ground to secure sculpture.

SNOWMAN (approximately 5′ tall)—MATERIALS: No. 10 galvanized steel wire, 7 lbs.; No. 20 wire, 1 lb.; garlands of plastic

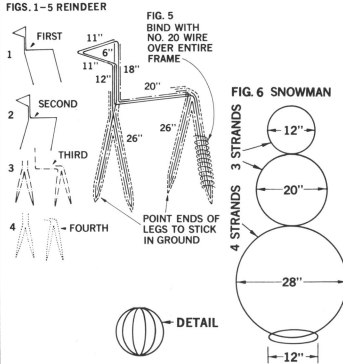

pine and holly; bee lights; 2″-wide red outdoor ribbon; an old hat.

DIRECTIONS: Our snowman is made with three spheres of No. 10 wire, stacked as in FIG. 6 and connected with No. 20 wire.

Top Sphere: Shape nine 12″-diameter wire circles. Join in groups of three, binding with No. 20 wire all around. Place circles inside each other to make a sphere of six equally-spaced segments and bind at top and bottom to hold (see details in FIG. 6).

Middle Sphere: Shape nine 20″-diameter circles; join and position as for Top Sphere.

Bottom Sphere: This time shape 12 circles,

each 28″ in diameter and join in groups of four. Bind and position as for Top Sphere. Stack the spheres and bind together, set on top of a 12″ diameter circle base. (made with four strands bound wire).

*To make arms*: Cut eight 31″ wires and bind in groups of four. Attach at "neck." Affix garlands to sculpture with No. 20 wire. Add lights and ribbon trim. Wire hat in place. Cut four 10″ lengths No. 10 wire and bend into arch shape. Slip over base circle and hammer into ground to secure sculpture.

## GLASS JAR LAMPS

MATERIALS (*for each lamp*): 18⅛″ high Mason jar, four-gallon size (Available from Libbey Glass); eight 15″ long peppermint poles and an assortment of smaller peppermint sticks and candies (Available from Bobs

*Color photo on page 66*

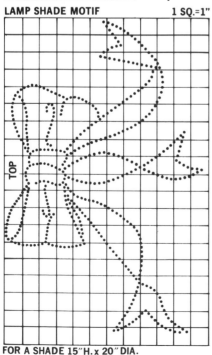

LAMP SHADE MOTIF          1 SQ.=1″

TOP

FOR A SHADE 15″H. x 20″ DIA.

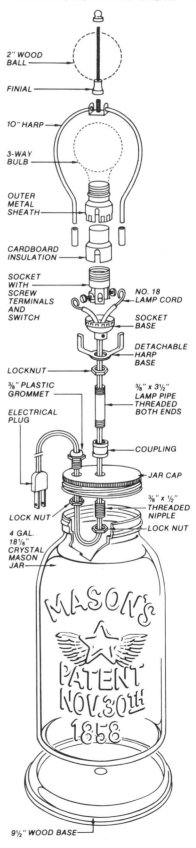

LAMP PARTS AND ASSEMBLY DIAGRAM

2″ WOOD BALL

FINIAL

10″ HARP

3-WAY BULB

OUTER METAL SHEATH

CARDBOARD INSULATION

SOCKET WITH SCREW TERMINALS AND SWITCH

NO. 18 LAMP CORD

SOCKET BASE

DETACHABLE HARP BASE

LOCKNUT

⅜″ PLASTIC GROMMET

⅜″ x 3½″ LAMP PIPE THREADED BOTH ENDS

ELECTRICAL PLUG

COUPLING

JAR CAP

⅜″ x ½″ THREADED NIPPLE

LOCK NUT

LOCK NUT

4 GAL. 18⅛″ CRYSTAL MASON JAR

MASON'S PATENT NOV. 30TH 1858

9½″ WOOD BASE

Candies Inc., Albany, Ga. 31706); white paper lampshade, 12″×20″×15″ high; 9½″ wooden lamp base; 2″ round wood ball; lamp fittings; red paint; drill for making holes in top of jar; brown paper; ice pick or awl.

DIRECTIONS:

1. Paint the lamp base and the round wood ball red. Let dry.

2. Place the large peppermint poles in the jar and fill between and on top of them with smaller candies.

3. Assemble the lamp as shown.

4. Following directions on page 140, enlarge the pattern on brown paper.

5. Tape the brown paper pattern to the lampshade, placing the bow design where you want it to be positioned on the shade. With an ice pick or awl, make holes through the brown paper and the lampshade about every ¼″ along the outline of the bow. Remove brown paper. Place the lampshade on the lamp; light will shine through the perforations.

## STAINED GLASS WINDOW DECORATION

Size depends on the size of your window. The wreath measures 26″ wide by 35″ long. The materials and the pattern given on the 2″ grids is for the above dimensions. To make larger or smaller patterns, make the size of the grid squares larger or smaller, adjusting the construction paper size accordingly.

GENERAL MATERIALS:

Two sheets of black construction paper— 30″×40″ for the wreath; one roll double-face transparent tape; X-acto knife No. 1 with extra blades; swivel knife; white or yellow carbon paper; heavy white tracing paper for the white portions of the wreath; one sheet each of colored cellophane as specified below (or gelatin sheets used by theaters to tint white spotlights, available at many photography shops); two black illustration boards.

Wreath Cellophane Colors: Red, orange, yellow, turquoise, chartreuse and emerald green.

GENERAL DIRECTIONS:

1. Following directions on page 140, enlarge the pattern onto brown paper the same size as the construction papers.

2. Cover one piece of construction paper with carbon paper and place pattern over it, edges

flush; trace pattern. Remove carbon and pattern.

3. Cover work area with a thick layer of newspapers to protect it.

1 SQ. = 2″

**BOW—RED; LEAVES—EMERALD GREEN
LEAF—CHARTREUSE; BERRIES—ASSORTED**

4. Place the blank construction sheet under the sheet with the tracing and pin all around edges. Place on newspaper.

5. Using X-acto knife and swivel knife, cut out all areas, including outer edges of wreath and ribbon, except the thick black outline shown in photo. Make sure you cut through both thicknesses of paper. This is a time-consuming job and must be done carefully, so allow yourself several hours to work quietly. You'll have a work of art.

6. When cutting is completed, set aside the bottom piece. What you have made is the "lead" portion of the stained glass window. The areas cut away will be filled in with colored "glass."

7. Tear narrow strips of transparent tape and, starting at the top of the design, place them on the lead, being sure to extend into the points of the holly leaves. Using the photo as a guide, place a piece of cellophane over the area and burnish with your thumbnail to press in place on the tape; trim off any excess color that extends beyond the lead. Add remaining pieces of color, one at a time, in same way, using tracing paper for white portions of wreath.

8. Place finished design over the bottom piece. With edges flush and cut-out areas matching perfectly, clip together at side edges and place strips of double-face tape along top edge of bottom piece. Press paper layer to bottom layer to make a firm bond. Remove clips.

9. Now, starting at the top again, lift the upper layer and repeat taping the lead areas on the bottom pieces as in Step 7, taping about 2″ across the design at a time. As you work downward, press and burnish the layers together.

## THREE-DIMENSIONAL FELT ORNAMENTS

MATERIALS: Foamcore board ³/₁₆″×30″ ×40″; 1 roll ¾″-wide black paper gift wrap ribbon; white fabric glue; felt squares or scraps in assorted colors; X-acto knife No. 1 with extra blades; tacks.

DIRECTIONS:

1. Following directions on page 140, enlarge patterns and cut out.

2. Trace *entire* shape onto foamcore once and cut out the ornament with the X-acto knife.

3. Trace felt appliqué areas onto various colors of felt and cut out.

4. Cut shaded portions from patterns and trace *twice* on foamcore; cut out. These are the dimensional pieces.

5. Glue felt to foamcore pieces, using photo as a guide.

### HOLLY LEAF PATTERNS

1 SQ. = 1″

LARGE    MEDIUM

SMALL

1 SQ. = 1″                    1 SQ. = 1″

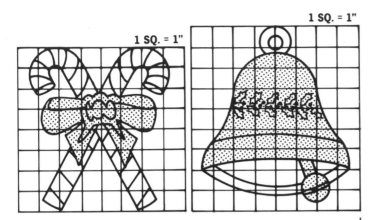

6. Tear paper ribbon into ³/₁₆″ strips and glue around edges of all pieces.

7. Stack and glue pieces together, sandwiching the full-size piece between the dimensional pieces.

8. Bind "sandwich" edges with a wide piece of black paper ribbon torn to correct width, extending at top to form a loop for hanging.

FELT HOLLY GARLAND—MATERIALS (*amounts depend on your window size*): ¼″ sisal rope measuring two times the width, plus two times the length of your window, plus 8″; one box each chartreuse and dark green chenille-wire pipe cleaners; one can green spray paint; four packages wired holly berries; 60″ wide felt—½ yd. each hunter green, Kelly green, chartreuse and lime; stiff cardboard; white fabric glue; nails and cup hooks. These materials were sufficient for our garland which measures 216″ long.

DIRECTIONS:

1. Following directions on page 140, enlarge the three sizes of holly leaf onto separate pieces of stiff cardboard and then cut out.

2. Trace patterns onto felt and cut out an equal amount of each size and color.

3. Two at a time, draw a line of white glue down the center of each leaf and glue to opposite ends of a pipe cleaner (alternating all the colors and sizes) to make holly sprays.

4. Spray rope with green paint.

5. When rope is dry, wrap holly sprays around rope at random, leaving 4″ bare at each end. Intersperse with clusters of holly berries.

6. Tack garland around window with bare ends overlapping at center bottom. Tuck under covered rope and secure with pipe cleaners.

## SURPRISE BALLS

MATERIALS: *For all surprise balls*: white glue; small toys, especially those that are round or square such as small ball or spring toy; flexible toys or candy, such as hand puppet, hair ribbons, jewelry; transparent tape; scissors. SANTA CLAUS: 1 roll white crepe paper streamers; red, white, pink, blue and black felt scraps; 10 cotton balls.

DIRECTIONS: *All Surprise Balls*: Starting with small round or square object, begin winding crepe paper around object, continually switching directions to form ball (like a ball of yarn). After first object is completely covered, put second one on and continue wrapping, trying to maintain as round a shape as possible. Continue with each object, cutting crepe paper and taping before starting with the next object. After last object is covered, tape end of crepe paper down. (*Note*: Don't worry if end product is not perfectly round; odd projections can be corrected or concealed by felt.) SANTA CLAUS: Follow directions, using white crepe paper. *Nose*: From red felt, cut out 1″ circle with attached top lip, about 2″×¼″ (see photo). Glue to center of face. *Cheeks*: From pink felt, cut out two 1¼″ circles and glue to either side of nose. *Eyes*: Cut two ovals, ½″×¼″, from blue felt, and glue slanting down, one over each cheek. Cut two ⅛″ circles from black felt and glue one in center of each eye. *Beard*: Glue 4 cotton balls onto face below lip. (Balls should be glued to each other as well as to face.) Glue 3 more below these, and 2 more below these, to make an inverse pyramid shape. *Cap*: Cut strip of red felt, 6″×12″. Wrap around top of head. Fold and glue to form peaked top. Glue 1 cotton ball to top. From white felt, cut out strip ½″ wide and long enough to wrap completely around base of cap. Glue onto cap, leaving very slight edge of red showing.

*Color photo on page 66*

## BASKET OF CANDY

MATERIALS: One 4″×6″ round straw basket with handle; 6″×6″×2″ piece of green Styrofoam; green floral wire, heavyweight; five 5″ spiral multi-colored suckers; artificial green floral leaves; green floral tape; red floral tape; ten 1″ pinecones; twelve 4″ pieces artificial Christmas greens; five 1¾″ fancy suckers with floral design; ten 1¼″ plain suckers, assorted colors; large and small gumdrops in assorted colors; jellied flower-shaped ½″ candies, assorted colors; eighteen 3″ candy canes (Available from Super Curly Q Pops, Creative Specialties, 7333 Coldwater Canyon, Unit 30, N. Hollywood, Ca. 91605); transparent cellophane tape; 54″ length of 1″ plaid ribbon.

DIRECTIONS: (*Note*: When arranging candy centerpiece, place longest candy flower stems in center top, medium stems in middle and shortest stems at basket edge. Also leave wrappers on suckers and candy canes to keep them fresh.) Cut Styrofoam to fit snugly into basket base. Cut floral wire into 7″ lengths; attach to suckers with floral tape to make long stems. Attach 2 leaves just below suckers to resemble flowers. Push the 5 spiral suckers in place (see photo); the center one should be the tallest with the 4 other spiral suckers equally spaced around the center one, slanting slightly outwards. Trim wires

as necessary to achieve a balanced arrangement. Push artificial greens and wired pinecones into Styrofoam as a filler around suckers, about 3″ high. Add plain colored suckers next, then flowered suckers. Push green floral wire into center of gumdrops and jellied candy flowers; scatter these throughout center-piece as desired. Cover wires for the candy canes with red floral tape; attach candy cane (leave wrappers on candy canes) to wire with transparent cellophane tape. Push wired candy canes into arrangement as needed. Cut 54″ length of ribbon in half. Tie a bow at the base of handle on each side of basket to finish.

## PINE CONE AND NUT CENTERPIECE

MATERIALS: Round disc of plywood, 12″ diameter; one 12″ diameter circle of felt for backing; one 3″ diameter circle of felt for top; Slomon's Quick Glue; Krylon Acrylic Spray Coating; Valspar brown stain; an assortment of nuts including acorns, horse chestnut (or regular store chestnuts), pine cones (1½ to 3″ or 4″ high; also some which have not opened), hazelnuts, walnuts and almonds.

DIRECTIONS: Stain the plywood disc brown. Allow to dry. Glue 12″ felt circle to bottom. Glue 3″ felt circle in center of top. Select the largest pine cones and form a circle around outside edge of plywood circle. Using glue sparingly. Next, glue a second circle of pine cones inside the first, leaving a 3″ circle for your candle. Pine cones should *not* be perfectly aligned. Now glue a third circle of pine cones on top of the first two. Let this set overnight. Now the build up: In between your pine cone circles, start to fill in with

smaller cones. As you look down, fill in spaces with the various nuts, small cones, etc. Let them set. If you wish, you can fill in the sides with nuts and acorns as you go around the wreath. When you are satisfied with the appearance of having filled in all voids, let it set overnight. Next, spray with 3 coats of Krylon Acrylic Spray Coating, allowing 1 hour between each coat.

## PASTA ANGEL AND ORNAMENTS

MATERIALS: *For Angel*: 12" Styrofoam cone; 3"-diameter Styrofoam ball; white glue; 5" square beige knit fabric; white felt scraps; shirt cardboard; straight pins; thin spaghetti; assorted fancy pastas; scissors; pencil; compass. *For Ornaments*: 3"-diameter Styrofoam balls; assorted small size pastas; thin wire; white glue.

DIRECTIONS: *Angel*: Cut off ¾" of cone tip. Glue ball to cut edge of cone; let dry. Stretch and pin fabric over front (face) area of ball. Cut off any excess fabric. Cut eye and mouth shapes of felt; glue to face. With pencil lines, divide cone vertically into quarters, making first line at center front. Glue band of fancy trimming pasta to this. Glue one piece of thin spaghetti to each of the other lines. (The piece will not be long enough to reach from neck to hem, but border at bottom and collar will cover the space.) Let dry. Working toward the center of each quarter, glue pieces of spaghetti parallel to the first ones. Gradually a "miter" will form at center of quarter and spaghetti must be broken to fit. Cover entire cone. Let dry overnight. Glue hem and collar trim in place. (We used "bows" and curly macaroni.) Cover hair area of head with rice pasta. Spread glue over small area at a time; sprinkle well with pasta; let dry; repeat. Cut 2 triangular arms out of cardboard. Cover with spaghetti on one side and about 2" up from bottom on reverse side. Add trim to edge (to match center of "robe"). Glue to sides of body. Glue on one pasta shell for each "hand."

*For halo*: Cut 4½"-diameter circle from cardboard; cut out 2½"-diameter concentric circle to make ring. Cover one side with spaghetti and pasta as shown in photo; glue to head.

*Ornaments*: Cut a 12" length of wire and push one end through the center of the Styrofoam

ball, leaving excess wire sticking out of one end. Working in small areas, and letting glue dry slightly as you go along, spread white glue on ball; stick pasta pieces onto ball. (Use a liberal amount of glue so that pasta does not slide off the round surface.) When entire surface is covered, hang ball by the wire to air-dry. If desired, glue additional pasta "bows" over the first layer.

## NOËL TABLECLOTH

Finished embroidered area measures approximately 16" from center to outer edge.

MATERIALS: Ready-made polyester/linen washable tablecloth or fabric to make tablecloth, size as desired; Size 2 crewel needle; DMC #5 cotton perlé, 1 each in the following colors: yellow, gold, salmon, pink, orange, red, maroon, yellow-orange; transfer pencil; large embroidery hoop; basting needle and thread; tracing paper for pattern; straight pins.

DIRECTIONS: *Enlarging and Transferring Pattern*: Fold fabric in half, lengthwise; press. Repeat for width. With pins, mark an 11⅝" square, using pressed folds as center guide. Baste square; remove pins. (This square will be guide for positioning and transferring motif.) Following directions on page 140, enlarge pattern; transfer onto tracing paper (design given repeats in quarters). Retrace this enlarged design on large sheet of tracing paper which has been folded in quarters; repeat original tracing in each of the quarters until design is complete, making sure front half of "Noël" matches back half where sections meet. Turn tissue over; on reverse side, redraw all lines with trans-

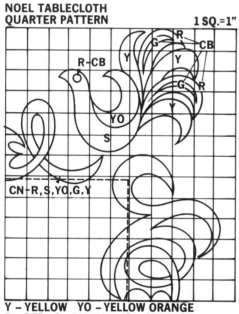

**NOEL TABLECLOTH QUARTER PATTERN**   1 SQ.=1"

Y – YELLOW   YO – YELLOW ORANGE
R – RED   S – SALMON   G – GOLD
CB – COLOR CHANGES ON OTHER BIRDS
CN – COLOR CHANGES ON OTHER NOELS

fer pencil. With this side down, center the pattern inside the basting lines on tablecloth. Pin securely to the right side of tablecloth. Pin in place around edges, smoothing paper out from center to remove any wrinkles or pleats. Press paper with hot iron in a circular motion to transfer the design to the fabric. Unpin and remove pattern. *To embroider:* Using hoop, embroider as follows (use photo and diagram as guides): Chain Stitch has been used throughout and should follow curves of all lines. Place fabric in embroidery hoop (since the design is large, you will have to work it a section at a time). With Chain Stitch (*see* BASIC EMBROIDERY STITCHES), embroider the birds. Each bird has a different color accent; use red, maroon, pink and orange for feather and eye. Eyes are 2 chain stitches sewn side by side. Colors on the words "Noël" have been worked in a similar sequence. For subtle shading, chain stitch one row each of yellow, gold, yellow-orange and salmon next to each other. Fill in what is left with bright color used in feathers and eye of adjacent bird. Press entire cloth on wrong side over towel or padding to finish.

## APPLIQUED TABLECLOTH AND NAPKINS

MATERIALS: Sandlewood cloth and napkins of desired size; wrapping paper; dressmaker's carbon and tracing wheel; scraps and small pieces of solid color percale or similar cotton-blend fabric, and of calico with tiny floral patterns; matching threads; yardstick; tailor's chalk; embroidery hoop (*this latter is optional*).

DIRECTIONS: Following the directions on page 140, enlarge and cut out the patterns for the appliqué motifs.

*Transferring the Designs:* Lay the cloth on the table, making sure it is centered exactly, with the overhang even all around. To keep the cloth from slipping, weight it with small heavy objects, moving them around as needed so they are out of the way as you work. Using a yardstick and pins, measure off and mark the exact center of each edge of the table top. From these marks, add pins (or baste) in a straight line 18″ long and perpendicular to the table edge.

*Note:* If you are decorating a cloth for a table that seats more than four, measure off and mark the center line of *each place setting area.*

Draw a pencil line down the middle of the Man and Woman patterns. Pin the patterns in place *(see photo)* with their feet on the table edge and their center lines about 9″ from the marked center line on the cloth. Trace the outline of each pattern with tailor's chalk. Remove the patterns.

Pin the Cherry Garland pattern in place with one end on the marked center line and the bottom cherry about ¼″ above the Woman's shoulder. Trace. Unpin pattern, reverse it and pin in place on the other side of the line. Trace again. Remove pattern. Pin and trace patterns in the other place setting areas.

Pin the Cherry Sprig pattern in one corner of each napkin; trace. Remove pattern. *Cutting and Sewing the Appliqués*: Using dressmaker's carbon and a tracing wheel, trace the separate parts of the enlarged patterns onto fabrics. *Cut the fabric ¼″ outside the traced lines*. Turning the edges under about ¼″, pin and baste the appliqué pieces to the tablecloth and napkins so that they cover the tracing lines. Remove cloth from table. With matching thread, blindstitch the edges of the appliqués. (*Note*: You may find it easier to work with the fabric held taut in an embroidery hoop.) Remove all the basting threads. Then steam-press the appliqués.

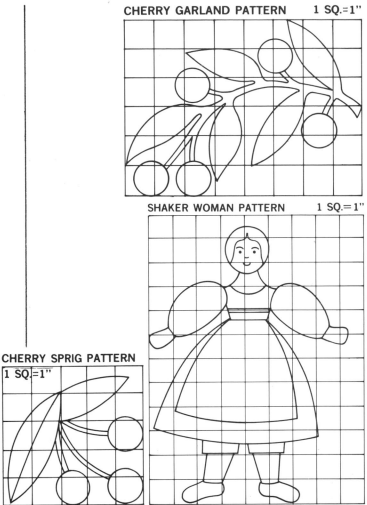

CHERRY GARLAND PATTERN    1 SQ.=1″

SHAKER WOMAN PATTERN    1 SQ.=1″

CHERRY SPRIG PATTERN
1 SQ.=1″

SHAKER MAN PATTERN    1 SQ.=1″

## ORGANDY ROSE CENTER PIECE AND TABLE CLOTH

### ORGANDY ROSE BUDS

**MATERIALS:** Ecru organdy 1 yd. 48″ wide will make about 26 buds; #16 gauge stem wire; ½″ masking tape; white floral tape.

**DIRECTIONS:** For *each bud*, cut a stem wire to desired length; bend a small hook at one end. Cut a *bias* strip of fabric 4¼″×12″. Cut a diagonal piece from one end so that one long edge of the strip measures 12″ and the other 8″. Lightly fold the 12″ edge down to the 8″ edge; do not crease the fold. Hold the straight end of the folded strip between the thumb and index finger of your *left* hand; with your *right* hand, wrap the strip loosely around the thumb and index finger to form a roll. Insert the *straight* end of the stem wire into the top of the bud; pull the wire through, hooking a piece of the center roll as you pull. Pinch the base of the roll together around wire; secure with masking tape. Wrap stem with white floral tape.

### LINEN AND LACE TABLECLOTH

**MATERIALS** *(for a 51″ square cloth)*: Ecru, 54″-wide Belgian linen, 1¼ yds.; 2½″-wide blond lace, 9 yds.; 1″-wide blond lace, 12 yds.;

¼″-wide red velvet ribbon, 3 yds. *(optional)*.

**DIRECTIONS:**
1. Cut four 20″ squares of linen. Press ⅛″ of each edge to the fabric right side. Pin narrow lace to the edges, covering 1″ of the fabric all around and mitering the corners; edgestitch in place.
2. Zigzag wide lace around squares, mitering corners.
3. Join two of these squares by edgestitching a strip of narrow lace between them; repeat with remaining squares. Now join the two pairs, also with narrow lace, to form one large square.
4. *Optional:* Thread red ribbon through the lace joining-strips, carefully cutting two threads on opposite sides of the lace center-square design to make the necessary openings. To decorate your table encircle a clear punch bowl with organdy rosebuds and baby's breath.

## ANGEL PLACE CARD HOLDERS

**MATERIALS:** One batch Basic Salt Dough (enough to make 4-5 angels); cookie sheet, lightly oiled; aluminum foil; nail or toothpick; garlic press; red poster paint; gold metallic paint; brushes; knife; shellac.

**DIRECTIONS:** Prepare BASIC SALT DOUGH, following directions on page 7. Roll 4 balls of dough, ¾″ in diameter, into long, tapered teardrop shapes. Curve slightly and place on cookie sheet, moistening edges where they join. Add a flattened ball at top for head. Make feet from 2 smaller balls,

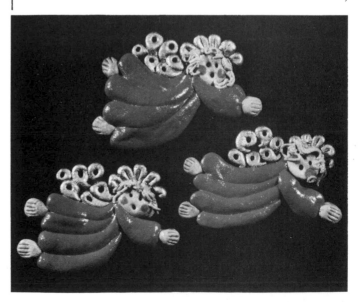

slightly elongated. Make indentations for toes with knife. (Moisten edges when joining to body.) Roll out a larger teardrop shape from ½″ ball for arm; moisten and lay on body. Attach a flattened ball of dough to end of arm with water, to form placecard rest. Place a folded piece of foil on this ball; add a smaller ball over foil for hand, using knife to form fingers. Make wings from small teardrops of dough, flattened, curved and joined to body with water. For halos, make dough ovals; indent at centers with knife. For hair, push small amount of dough through garlic press; moisten area around face and add strands. Use nail or toothpick to make holes for eyes and mouth and in each of the shapes forming wings. Bake at 325° for about 1 hour, or until rock hard. Cool; remove foil ball from between hands. Paint, leaving face, hands and feet natural, if you wish. Dilute red paint with water for cheeks. Use gold paint on wings and halos. Coat all exposed surfaces with shellac, for a permanent seal.

## CALICO "WREATH" TABLE SETTINGS
### PLACEMATS
Finished size: 14″ diameter circle.

MATERIALS: *For 4 placemats*: ¾ yard 40″ wide fleecy interfacing; 1 yard 44″ wide green calico print; ¼ yard 44″ wide white cotton fabric; white thread; needle; straight pins; compass; pencil; paper for making patterns.

DIRECTIONS: *For each placemat*: Cut one 14″ diameter circle of interfacing, one 14″ diameter circle calico. Cut 1″ wide strips of calico along the bias and stitch together to form a strip 38″ long. (Bias strips will form mat borders.) Trace a 7¾″ diameter circle onto white fabric; cut out ¼″ outside drawn line. *To assemble*: Pin calico and interfacing circles together (wrong side of calico to interfacing). Baste around edges. In center of calico, draw a 7½″ diameter circle. Machine stitch along drawn circle line. Machine stitch over drawn circle on white fabric. Turn under on stitching line, clipping curves to ease folds. Baste turned edges down. Pin wrong side of white circle to stitched circle on calico; slipstitch all around. Remove basting. *To finish*: Pin bias strip to outer edge of calico, right sides together, easing to fit. Stitch ¼″ in from edge. Turn bias under edge of mat (to interfacing). Turn raw bias edge under;

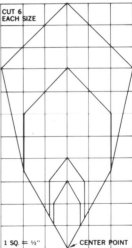

CUT 6 EACH SIZE

1 SQ. = ½″  CENTER POINT  PETALS CALICO TABLE SETTINGS

slipstitch to interfacing.
### FLOWERS
MATERIALS: *For each flower*: ¼ yard 38″ wide red calico print; three 6″ long white pipe cleaners; ¼″ diameter plastic drinking straw; 45″ length thin wire; green thread; needle; fabric glue; pencil; compass; paper for patterns. (*Note*: You may wish to vary flowers by using contrasting calicoes for petals, and by adding extra rounds of petals. Our photo shows some flowers made in 2 and some in 3 layers of contrasting colors.)

DIRECTIONS: Following directions on page 140, enlarge patterns for two largest petals. Cut out pattern pieces. *For each flower*: Cut two 8″ diameter circles from calico; cut two 11″ diameter circles. Fold one 8″ circle into quarters; mark center point; unfold. Match inside point of smaller petal pattern to center point of circle. Trace around pattern. Move pattern around center until you have traced 6 evenly spaced petals. Pin to unmarked 8″ circle, wrong sides together. Draw 3 "vein" lines running through center from tip to tip of opposite petals. On each petal, stitch 2 lines in green thread (one on each side of "vein" line), tapering both lines to a point at outside petal tip. Brush fabric glue between layers of petals except within "vein" lines; let dry. Set machine on close zigzag and stitch along petal outlines in green thread. Trim away excess fabric close to zigzag lines. Fold flower in quarters and clip a ⅛ wide hole in center. Cut three 6″ pieces of wire; slide wire through center holes into "veins." Repeat entire process with 11″ circles, largest petal pattern and 9″ pieces of wire. *To assemble*: Lay 8″ petals atop 11″ ones. Fold 3 pipe cleaners in half and push them (folded side down) through 8″, then 11″ flower centers, so they all fit snugly into straw. Leave about 1″ ends above flower; spread ends slightly. For a longer stem, crease bottom of first straw and slide it into a second one.

NAPKIN RINGS

MATERIALS: *For 4 rings*: ¼ yard 38″ wide red calico; twelve 6″ pipe cleaners; green thread; compass; pencil; paper for pattern.

DIRECTIONS: Enlarge and trace 2 smallest petal patterns onto paper; cut out pattern pieces. From calico, cut two 3″ diameter circles and two 4″ diameter circles. Make flowers as outlined in FLOWER DIRECTIONS, omitting "veins," wires and straws. Loosely braid 3 pipe cleaners. Slip ends up through 4″, then 3″ flower, leaving ½″ length above flower. Twist and spread pipe cleaner ends. Shape loop below flower into a ring. Slip napkin into ring and place at top of mat to resemble wreath.

## CAROLLERS

MATERIALS: Egg-shaped hosiery containers; pipe cleaners; small jar lids; paper bag; birthday candles; Styrofoam or aluminum foil; construction paper; cardboard; white glue; felt-tip marking pens; assorted felt scraps; assorted scraps of ribbon, lace and trim.

DIRECTIONS: *For each Caroller*: glue both halves of hosiery container together; let dry. Glue the lid from a small jar to the smaller half of each egg for a stand.

*Men*: Make men's hats from cylinders of felt with the tops slightly wider than the bottoms. Cut a circle of felt to cover the hole in the top and glue in place. Do the same for the brim. Trim with holly leaves cut from felt, if you wish. Men's scarves are made from strips of felt. Mittens are cut from felt and glued onto pieces of pipe cleaner. Glue pipe cleaner arms to the egg, bending arms as desired. Hair, sideburns and facial features are drawn on the eggs with felt-tip marker.

*Women*: The women's hats are made from felt the same way as the men's, except they are wider at the base and smaller at the top. Hats can be trimmed with fuzzy piping to simulate fur. Make dresses by wrapping two pieces of wide velvet ribbon around the egg. Capes are cut from felt, trimmed and glued to the egg. Make hair from narrow strips of felt or construction paper, curled by running between a scissors blade and thumb. Glue in place. Carollers' song books are made from cardboard and glued to mittens. Candles can be supported by small glued-on piece of Styrofoam or aluminum foil between pipe cleaner arms.

*Color photo on page 66*

## POPCORN MANTELS

Make any mantel festive with popcorn strings, punctuated at both ends with big clusters of candycanes and ribbons.

## ADVENT CALENDAR

MATERIALS: ¾ yard 44"-wide linen or linen-like fabric (measures 25"×36"); one 9"×12" piece felt in contrasting color; size 3 or 4 embroidery needle; transfer pencil; tissue paper; stencil lettering guide for 1" Roman letters and numbers; 24 (1"-diameter) off-white plastic curtain rings; 1 thin-pointed permanent felt-tip pen (to outline stencil numbers on felt); basting thread; sewing needle; pinking shears; frame; quilting Pellon®; white glue; staple gun or carpet tacks; two 18" and two 32" canvas stretchers; embroidery hoop; 24 pieces wrapped candy; scraps of embroidery floss; 6-strand DMC embroidery floss in the following amounts and colors.

*For Flowers*:

| No. of Skeins | Color | Diagram Key Letter |
|---|---|---|
| 3 | Gold | N |
| 2 | Medium Brown | O |
| 1 | Light Beige | P |
| 1 | Gray | R |
| 3* | Yellow | S |
| 4 | Dark Brown | T |

*Enough for flowers and angels.

*For Angels*:

| No. of Skeins | Color | Diagram Key Letter |
|---|---|---|
| 1 | Salmon Pink | A |
| 1 | Light Pink | B |
| 1 | Bright Orange | C |
| 1 | Medium Orange | D |
| 1 | Light Orange | E |
| 1 | Medium Pink | F |
| 1 | Dusty Pink | G |
| 1 | Bright Pink | H |
| 1 | Dusty Dark Red | J |
| 2 | Light Purple | K |
| 2 | Medium Purple | L |
| 3 | Dark Purple | M |

DIRECTIONS: Baste rectangle on linen to measure 11¼"×25¼". Do this along weave of linen (squarely). Enlarge designs onto tissue paper, following directions on page 140, and trace designs onto tissue paper. Turn tissue over; on reverse side, redraw all lines with transfer pencil. With marked side down, place patterns on linen following photo for placement of angels. Half patterns given for flower border must be "flopped" for borders.

24

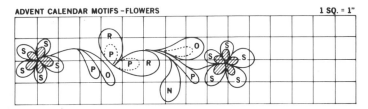

ADVENT CALENDAR MOTIFS—FLOWERS          1 SQ. = 1"

ANGELS

Working in sections (as you will use patterns more than once), pin each pattern in place; press paper with hot iron in a circular motion to transfer the design to fabric; unpin and remove fabric; repeat until entire design is transferred.

*To Embroider*: Using all 6 strands of floss, embroider designs following diagram and Materials chart for colors. Only three stitches have been used: Chain, Back Stitch and Satin Stitch (*see* BASIC EMBROIDERY STITCHES). Use Satin and Back Stitches for flowers and wings, Chain for robes. Sprinkle stars around with 4 short stitches.

*Numbers*: Trace numbers (1 through 24) from stencil sheet onto felt with felt-tipped pen. *Important*: Turn stencil over and trace numbers *backwards* so pen marks will be on back of numbers. Also, close all breaks on stencil as you trace. To position numbers, baste a line across 12" width of fabric 12¼" down from top basted line. Baste lines down both sides of 25¼" length 1½" in from each side. Space numbers 11 to 15 evenly across width on basted line using side lines as edges. Glue on with white glue. Place other numbers in rows 2" apart and aligned with center row. (Basting lines throughout help in positioning.) See photo to position numbers 1, 2 and 24. Following basting line, work border in gold as single row of Back Stitches. Work stars. Press embroidery on wrong side, face

down, on towel. Remove all basting stitches. Press Pellon. Staple or tack it evenly on canvas stretchers pulling taut and folding or clipping off corners. Center embroidery over stretched Pellon and staple to Pellon, making sure fabric is pulled taut and smooth. (Work from center to edges, pulling evenly on all 4 sides and turning frequently.) Position and sew on plastic rings below numerals with floss through Pellon backing. Tie candy to rings. Frame as desired.

**BOTTLE CAP ADVENT CALENDAR**
MATERIALS needed are given in order used in Directions below.
DIRECTIONS: Use photo as a guide. *Pine Board* 12"×24"—cut top and bottom edges in curved shape; sand edges; glue decorative molding to side edges; coat with gesso (a white liquid sealer); paint red. Attach sawtooth hanger to back.
*Christmas tree:* Cut from green and black felt and glue to board; paste large gold Christmas medallion at tree top, and smaller ones at random; screw 23 eyelets through felt into board, spacing them as in photo; screw 3 eyelets to board alone around tree top.
*Angels:* From felt, cut 2 angels; add magic marker strokes for features, hair and wings;

glue to board at right and left of tree top.
*Assorted sizes bottle caps and jar lids:* Punch a small hole in the center of the lip; insert 1½" copper wire and twist ends, leaving a ¼" loop on top; spray with gold paint inside and out. When dry, glue gold foil strips around lips inside, glue felt circles with small Christmasy pictures pasted to center. On outside, paint in bright colors. Paste on gold foil medallions and black numbers, 1-24, in center of medallions. With red string, tie lids to eyelets (largest in center), with numbered side up; on each day of Advent, reverse one lid to show picture inside.

## ANGEL BANNER
MATERIALS: Large embroidery hoop; white linen fabric, 36" square; Size 2 crewel needle; 6-strand embroidery floss: 2 skeins red, 2 skeins blue, 6 skeins purple; 100% wool, 3-strand crewel yarn (use 2 of 3 strands): 3 skeins dk. pink, 3 skeins med. pink, 2 skeins lt. pink, 2 skeins gold, 2 skeins red orange, 3 skeins orange, 1 skein brown; basting thread; sewing needle; knitting yarn for fringe; 36" square white fabric for backing; 30" dowel; paper for pattern; dressmaker's carbon.
DIRECTIONS: Following directions on page 140, enlarge and trace design onto tissue paper. Transfer angel onto center of fabric with dressmaker's carbon, following grain. Embroider design (*see* BASIC EMBROIDERY STITCHES), following stitch diagram, using 2 of 3 strands of wool and all 6 strands of floss, same needle for both. Colors shown on diagram also delineate floss from yarn, as both are worked in different colors. Work angel, then borders. *To back embroidery:* Lay embroidery wrong side up on a thick towel. Fold side edges over (to wrong side) ¼" out from embroidered borders; press. Baste, then stitch backing fabric to linen along sides, right sides together. Stitch backing to top edge 2" above top row of border embroidery; turn right side out. *To make dowel casing:* Turn top under 2"; tack firmly. If you wish, paint dowels and attach decorative knobs; insert into casing. *To make fringe along bottom border:* Using 1 skein (4 ozs. or less) 4-ply orlon acrylic knitting yarn, cut pieces to 14" lengths. Cut as needed. Sew to bottom edge of finished hanging with tapestry needle.

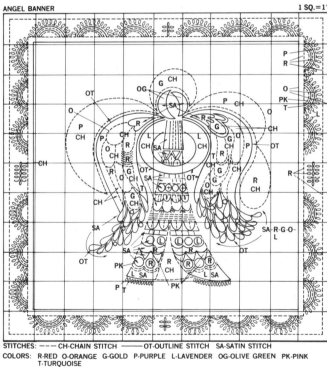

ANGEL BANNER     1 SQ.=1"

STITCHES: ------ CH-CHAIN STITCH   ―――― OT-OUTLINE STITCH   SA-SATIN STITCH
COLORS: R-RED O-ORANGE G-GOLD P-PURPLE L-LAVENDER OG-OLIVE GREEN PK-PINK T-TURQUOISE

Use this yarn also to make hanger. We used three 144" lengths of yarn braided together.

## NEEDLEPOINT FAMILY
Finished size measures 16"×18".
MATERIALS: 20"×22" piece of 13 mesh mono canvas (larger or smaller mesh canvas will mean different size piece); masking tape; size 18 tapestry needle; ordinary sewing needle;

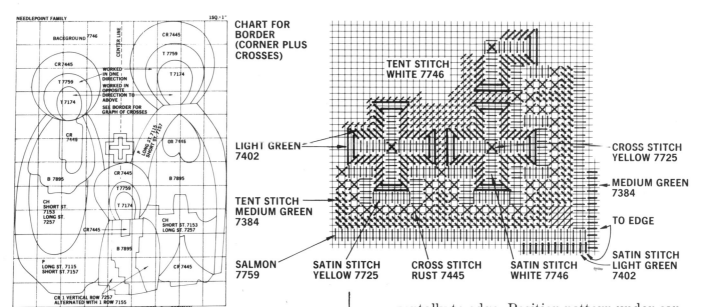

**NEEDLEPOINT FAMILY** 1 SQ. = 1"

BACKGROUND 7746
CR 7445
T 7759
T 7174
CENTER LINE
WORKED IN ONE DIRECTION
WORKED IN OPPOSITE DIRECTION TO ABOVE
SEE BORDER FOR GRAPH OF CROSSES
CR 7445
T 7759
T 7174
CR 7449
OR 7445
B 7895
CR 7445
T 7759
T 7174
B 7895
LONG ST. 7115 SHORT ST. 7157
CH SHORT ST. 7153 LONG ST. 7257
CR 7445
CH SHORT ST. 7153 LONG ST. 7257
B 7895
P LONG ST. 7115 SHORT ST. 7157
CR 7445
CR 1 VERTICAL ROW 7257 ALTERNATED WITH 1 ROW 7155
CR — CROSS  T — TENT  B — BUTTONHOLE  CH — CHEVRON  P — PARISIAN

**CHART FOR BORDER (CORNER PLUS CROSSES)**

TENT STITCH WHITE 7746
LIGHT GREEN 7402
TENT STITCH MEDIUM GREEN 7384
SALMON 7759
SATIN STITCH YELLOW 7725
CROSS STITCH RUST 7445
SATIN STITCH WHITE 7746
CROSS STITCH YELLOW 7725
MEDIUM GREEN 7384
TO EDGE
SATIN STITCH LIGHT GREEN 7402

*Color photo on page 66*

gold-colored sewing thread; permanent ink felt-tipped markers; pencil; white paper for pattern; DMC tapestry wool, in the following colors and amounts (*Note:* Yarn amounts listed are for 13 mesh mono canvas.): 1 skein each of #7153 pink, #7174 tan, #7257 dark purple, #7155 hot pink, 2 skeins each of #7895 medium purple, #7157 dark pink, #7115 burgundy, #7725 yellow, 3 skeins each of #7759 salmon, #7384 medium green, 4 skeins each of #7445 rust, #7402 light green, 18 skeins #7746 white; 1 skein Schurer #3/6 gold thread, or any gold yarn. *To finish:* 16″ × 18″ wood canvas stretchers; staple gun or hammer and carpet tacks; frame, as desired. (*Note:* A needlepoint stand is recommended.)
**DIRECTIONS:** Following directions on page 140, enlarge pattern onto white paper. Mark outlines and center lines with heavy pencil line or felt-tipped marker. Tape edge of canvas. Mark center lines vertically and hori-

zontally to edge. Position pattern under canvas, centering it widthwise with more space at the top than at the bottom (see photo). Trace design onto canvas with felt-tipped marker. Attach piece to needlepoint stand. Work figures first, following stitch diagram. Work crosses along center line, starting above and below child (see border diagram). Work one cross completely, counting carefully; when one is counted out, others will follow easily, 1 mesh apart. Use photo as a guide to the number of crosses in frame around family. Work background in Continental (tent) Stitch (*see* **BASIC NEEDLE-POINT STITCHES**), continuing it into and around crosses. Finally, couch gold thread around figures, outlining the areas of different stitches in and around family. Use ordinary gold sewing thread as anchoring thread. *To finish:* If no frame is used, block canvas, either professionally or using blocking kit. If frame is used, there is no need to block canvas. Mark top and outer side centers on stretcher strips. Assemble frame corners. Use center lines on canvas to match marks on frame and tack or staple needlepoint in place; pull taut, alternating on all 4 sides until piece is evenly stretched.

## RAINBOW BANNER

Finished size: 35″×60″
**MATERIALS:** 36″-wide nylon\* fabric (or cotton and cotton blends) in the following amounts and colors: 1¾ yards light blue, ⅜ yard dark green, ⅛ yard yellow ochre, ¾

yard apple green, ⅜ yard brown, ⅜ yard pink, ⅜ yard gold, ½ yard red, ½ yard orange, ⅜ yard blue, ⅜ yard purple; 6½ yards black polyester foldover braid; 1 spool each dark and light nylon thread; scissors; zigzag sewing machine; straight pins; dressmaker's carbon; paper for pattern.
*If nylon fabric is used, banner may be hung outdoors.

DIRECTIONS: Following directions on page 140, enlarge pattern onto paper with white dressmaker's carbon. Cut each pattern piece separately. When using patterns to cut fabric, cut along dotted lines where indicated to provide overlaps for stitching the pieces together. *Sky:* Cut light blue to 3′×5′ rectangle; cut bottom so that it extends beyond the top line of orange. *Rainbow:* Pin red stripe onto blue sky in place and sew down along top edge of red. *Note:* All pieces are stitched together with close machine zigzag. Cut orange nylon as on pattern, extending to overlap yellow, as shown. Pin on top of red and sew. Repeat for yellow, green and blue. The bottom color (purple) should be cut exactly as in the pattern; stitch down both top and bottom lines. Cut gold curve exactly as on pattern; pin; stitch only top line. Pink mountains below it should extend to slip under the gold curve above and under brown curve below. Pin and stitch bottom edge of gold to pink. Cut brown exactly as on pattern; pin and stitch top line only. Fit the green up under brown, leaving enough fabric at the bottom to extend into area that will be yellow ochre. Pin and stitch bottom brown line. Cut the dark green 1″ longer than on pattern. Place on bottom of banner. Pin and stitch across bottom and then both sides at extreme edge to hold together. Cut yellow ochre band as on pattern and place over gap between dark green and apple green (it should cover raw edges of both). Pin; sew along both edges of yellow ochre strip. *To finish:* Encase entire border of banner with the foldover braid, pinning and sewing a few inches at a time. Cut 4 pieces of foldover braid 5″. Iron out the fold. On each piece, sew the raw edges together. Place two of these loops at the top corners of the banner and the other two at 10¾″ in from each edge, tucking raw edges of loops under as you pin. Stitch down all four loops very well, reinforcing

them and making sure tucked-under raw edges have been caught in stitching. *To hang:* slip a dowel through loops, or tack the banner to wall through the undersides of the braid loops.

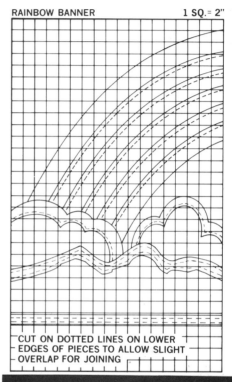

RAINBOW BANNER                1 SQ.= 2″

CUT ON DOTTED LINES ON LOWER EDGES OF PIECES TO ALLOW SLIGHT OVERLAP FOR JOINING

# Stockings to Stuff

## CROCHETED STOCKING

MATERIALS: Coats & Clark's "Red Heart" Knitting Worsted, 4 ply ("Tangle-Proof" Pull-Out Skeins): 6 oz. of Scarlet, 3 oz. of White; crochet hook, size J.

DIRECTIONS FOR STOCKING FRONT: Crochet with double yarn throughout. Working with red yarn, ch 18.

*1st row:* Sc in 2nd ch from hook, * sc in next ch; repeat from * across chain; ch 1, turn.

*2nd row:* 2 sc in first sc, * sc in next sc; repeat from * across row to within last sc; 2 sc in last sc; ch 1, turn.

*3rd row:* Sc across row to within last sc; 2 sc in last sc; ch 1, turn.

*4th through 9th rows:* Repeat 2nd and 3rd row 3 times (29 sc).

*10th and 11th rows:* Work even.

*12th row:* Dec 1 sc at end of row.

*13th row:* Work even.

*14th row:* Dec 1 sc at end of row.

*15th row:* Dec 1 sc at beg of row.

*16th and 17th rows:* Repeat 14th and 15th rows.

*18th row:* Sc to within last 7 scs (17 sc). Work 21 more rows across the 17 sc. Break off red yarn and fasten ends. Attach white yarn. Work 4 rows of dc. Break off white.

*Fringe:* Cut 4" lengths of white yarn by loosely wrapping yarn around 2" wide cardboard and cutting at one edge. Fold 3 strands (4" each) in half. Insert crochet hook under dc in 1st row of dc and through loop of fringe; draw loop under dc to right side, draw ends through loop and pull ends tightly. Work 3-strand fringe on each dc of the cuff's 4 rows. *Stocking Back:* Work same as front, but work fringe on opposite side.

*Finishing:* Sew seams of cuff together. Join remaining edges: Use double red yarn and work 1 row of sc through double thickness of stocking. Finish with 1 row of sc with white yarn.

*To Hang:* With double red yarn, make a chain 26". Fold in half. Attach folded chain to top of stocking back seam so that hanger loop measures 3½". Tie the remaining part of chain into a big bow; hang stocking.

## BAROQUE STOCKING

MATERIALS: ⅔ yd. red velvet; ½ yd. white felt; dressmaker's carbon paper; straight pins; pencil; paper for pattern; red thread; white thread; scissors.

DIRECTIONS: Following directions on page 140, enlarge and cut out stocking pattern with designs. Cut out two stocking pieces in red velvet and one in white felt. Pin felt stocking piece to right side of one of the red velvet stocking pieces. Turn these two pinned

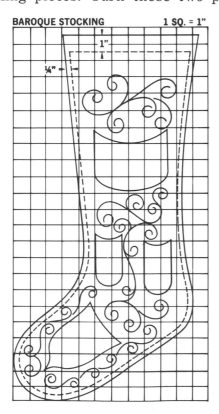

*Color photo on page 67*

pieces over; cover with dressmaker's carbon. Place paper stocking pattern over the carbon and pin through to the fabric. Trace design. Remove carbon and pattern. Sew with running stitch from this wrong side, following design tracing. Make sure tension is proper so that other side (bobbin side), which will be the exposed, right side of stocking, will show proper stitch tension. Do not stitch along top of pockets. Unpin, turn over, and cut along both sides of stitching, forming tracery scrolls. Cut around outside of pocket shapes only, to form the pockets. Pin right sides of both red velvet stocking pieces together. Sew together with ¼" seam, leaving top open. Turn right side out. Turn top edge under 1" and machine stitch two rows of stitching. Add white felt loop for hanging.

## RIBBON STOCKING

MATERIALS: ⅔ yd. unbleached muslin (or use good portion of discarded sheet); ⅔ yd. lining (taffeta, satin, etc.); ⅓ yd. red velveteen; gold middy braid (approximately 9 yds.); assorted ribbons in ¼", ½" and 1" widths (yardage varies with proportion of widths used; remnants of rayon/polyester seam binding can be used with the ribbons); thread to match velveteen and lining; straight pins; needle; scissors; pencil; paper for pattern.

DIRECTIONS: Following directions on page 140, enlarge pattern and transfer to paper. Cut out patterns. Using pattern, cut two muslin stocking pieces. Place both pieces of muslin,

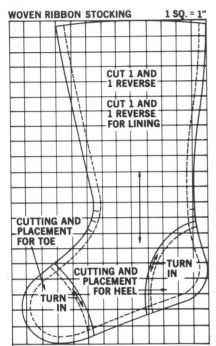

**WOVEN RIBBON STOCKING**      1 SQ. = 1"

CUT 1 AND
1 REVERSE

CUT 1 AND
1 REVERSE
FOR LINING

CUTTING AND
PLACEMENT
FOR TOE

CUTTING AND
PLACEMENT
FOR HEEL

TURN
IN

TURN
IN

*Color photo on page 67*

right side up, on a flat surface. Beginning at center, lengthwise lay ribbons and middy braid adjacent to each other and parallel to first ribbon so that entire stocking is covered. Cover both sides in exactly the same pattern of ribbons. Pin both ends of each ribbon to the stocking. Baste ribbons down at top edge; leave pins at bottom. Beginning just above ankle, weave ribbons and middy braid crosswise, pinning at both ends. Stitch ends of ribbons on one side. Adjust tension

where necessary and replace remaining pins with basting stitches. Using patterns, cut two toes and two heels from red velveteen. Place in position and pin. Turn in the edges indicated and stitch invisibly to stocking. Baste outer edge to stocking. Place stocking pieces right sides together and sew along stitching line. Leave top edge open. Turn right side out. Adjust any ribbons that become disarranged. Using pattern, cut two stocking pieces from lining. Sew lining pieces together, leaving top edge open. Do not turn. Insert into stocking. Baste lining to stocking at top edge. For cuff, cut velveteen 20" × 9½". Place right side against outside of stocking with one long edge even with top of stocking and stitch to stocking along top edge. Bind other long edge with ribbon. Overlap short ends of cuff, turn in raw edge and stitch. Bring bound edge up and just inside stocking; stitch. Sew loop of middy braid inside cuff as hanger.

## ICE SKATE STOCKING

This ice skate stocking is made with a No. 6 rug punch needle. With it you can punch long loops, indicated by the wavy lines in the pattern, and short loops, indicated by the straight lines. Instructions come with the needle.

MATERIALS: Red burlap 12" × 16" (bind the edges with masking tape); rug or craft yarn: royal blue, 11 yds., chartreuse, 6 yds., white 30 yds. (amounts are approximate); iron-on interfacing, 10" × 14"; red cotton fabric for backing, 10" × 14"; No. 6 rug punch needle and yarn needle; black felt-tipped marker.

DIRECTIONS: Following directions on page 140, enlarge and trace the design on burlap, using a black felt-tipped marker. Leave a 2" margin outside the grid. *To punch the design:* You are working from the back. The loops you punch will come out on the opposite, or right, side of the burlap. Start with royal blue. Use the short loop for blade of the ice skate and the blue line at the top of the stocking. Use the long loop for the line at the top of the shoe, the heel line and the border around the shoe lace. (The shoe lace will come later.) Next, punch the chartreuse; short loop for the line in the skate blade and the heel, long loop for the two chartreuse lines at the top of the stocking. Now outline and fill in the ice

ICE SKATE STOCKING                    1 SQ. = 1"

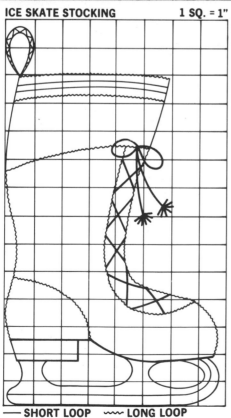

— SHORT LOOP    ∿∿∿ LONG LOOP

skate shoe with long loops of white. Add one row of short white loops to the border at the top of the stocking. When you have finished punching, check for skimpy spots and add a few more punches of the proper colors, if necessary. *The shoe lace:* Use a generous yard of blue yarn. Thread your yarn needle. Start on the right side of the burlap at the top of the shoe. Leave 6″ of yarn hanging loose and sew 5 X's, ending up back at the top of the shoe with the other loose end. Make pompons with two small loops of chartreuse and knot them to the ends of the blue yarn shoe laces. Tie a bow. *To finish the stocking:* Iron on interfacing to the wrong side of the burlap to keep loops from pulling out. Place red cotton backing on top of the right side of the punched design. Pin and stitch, being careful not to catch the shoe lace or long loops in the seam. Leave top open. Fold forward and hem the top. Turn stocking right side out. Make a loop to hang the stocking by braiding together 10″ strands of each color yarn. Attach to top back of the stocking.

## CROSS STITCH STOCKINGS

*Note:* These stocking were embroidered using knitting basket scraps. The Materials list below gives exact yardages, but you may wish to vary colors according to yarn scraps you have on hand.

MATERIALS: *For each stocking:* 23″ × 12″ piece of burlap in desired color. *Note:* Look for a burlap with a fairly even weave; ours was 12 threads to the inch. 23″ × 12″ piece green cotton fabric for stocking back; two 23″×12″ pieces white cotton fabric for lining; sewing thread; tailor's chalk; tapestry needle; knitting worsted in the following yardages and colors: *For Poinsettia stocking:* 28 yards blue, 22 yards scarlet, 3 yards dark green, 3 yards kelly green, ½ yard yellow. *For Ornament stocking:* 27 yards yellow, 13 yards scarlet, 9 yards cranberry, 1 yard dark green 2½ yards white. *For Candle stocking:* 33 yards kelly green, 12 yards white, 2½ yards pale yellow, 7 yards tan, 2½ yards dark green, ½ yard dark brown, ¼ yard orange.

DIRECTIONS: Following directions on page 140, enlarge and trace pattern for stocking outline onto paper, marking border and central design shapes as shown. Using tailor's chalk, trace pattern and markings onto bur-

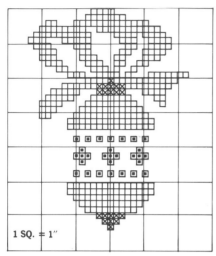

1 SQ. = 1"

**CROSS STITCH STOCKING**　　　　　　　　　1 SQ. = 1"

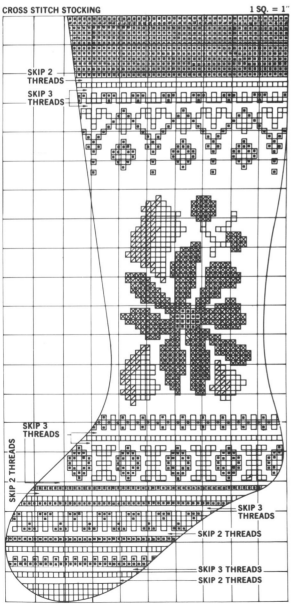

SKIP 2 THREADS

SKIP 3 THREADS

SKIP 3 THREADS

SKIP 2 THREADS

SKIP 3 THREADS

SKIP 2 THREADS

SKIP 3 THREADS

SKIP 2 THREADS

*Color photo on page 67*

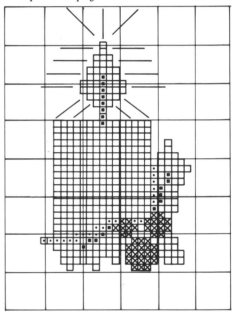

lap. Stay stitch around all edges of burlap just outside pattern, but do not cut out stocking shape. Mark design shapes and positions with loose basting, counting stitches and skipped threads for even design. When basting is completed, remove paper pattern. *To embroider:* Using Cross Stitch (*see* BASIC EMBROIDERY STITCHES) and the photo as a guide, work each stitch over two threads of your burlap. Do not make knots; catch yarn under stitches on back of work. Due to the irregularity of burlap weave, some Cross Stitches may fall outside the stocking outline; if so, fill in stitches to reach outline. Work borders first, then the outlined shapes, counting stitches as in diagram. *Finishing:* Stay stitch around stocking just outside outline; cut out stocking shape adding ½" seam allowance on all edges. Place embroidered piece face down and iron, using damp cloth. Using stocking pattern, cut 1 stocking back and 2 lining pieces, leaving ½″ seam allowance all around on each piece. Sew lining pieces together, leaving top open. Right sides together, sew stocking back to front, leaving top open; turn. Insert lining into stocking. Turn top raw edges of stocking and lining under (both to center, between them). Slipstitch top edges of stocking and lining closed. Press finished stocking. *For hangers:* Braid 3 strands of yarn together; tie yarn braid in a bow; tack firmly to top of stocking with sewing thread.

## DELFT CHRISTMAS STOCKINGS

MATERIALS: 45″ linen or linen-weave fabric, navy or royal blue and white (1/3 yard for 1 boot, ¼ yard for 1 cuff); 1/3 yard SiBonne for lining 1 boot; scissors; pins, thread; tissue tracing paper; tape; pencil; dressmaker's carbon paper and tracing wheel; embroidery needle, No. 5; embroidery hoop. Six-strand DMC embroidery floss in the following colors: dark blue; medium blue; light blue; bright green; medium green; light green; white; yellow.

DIRECTIONS: *Boot:* Following the directions on page 140, enlarge boot pattern onto tracing paper, adding ⅜″ seam allowance on all sides. (If you plan to use boot pattern more than once, use brown wrapping paper.) Fold 1/3 yard of linen fabric in half the long way; cut. Position boot pattern on ½ of linen; pin and

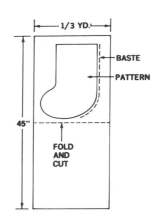

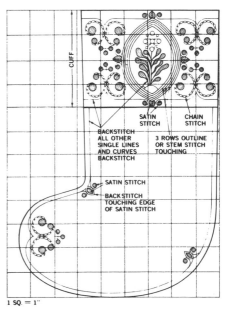

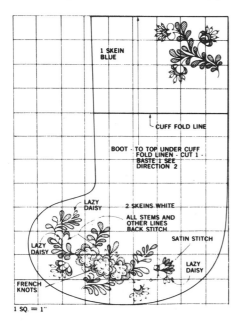

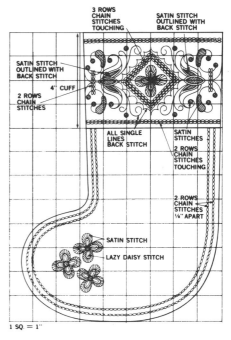

baste around outline with contrasting sewing thread. Do not cut out. Remove pattern and pin to other half of fabric. Cut this piece out. Embroider design on uncut piece of linen. (Enlarge design from grid.) Using dressmaker's carbon and tracing wheel, transfer design onto fabric. Thread embroidery needle with 6 strands of floss and use embroidery hoop. Embroider design (*see* **BASIC EMBROIDERY STITCHES**): Press on wrong side, with embroidery face down on terry towel. Trim boot along outside basting line. Using boot pattern, cut 2 pieces of lining material. Stitch around sides, with right sides together, leaving top open. Clip inner curves; press seams open. Do not turn. Join lining to boot, matching seams, with open seams meeting. Set aside until cuff is made. *Cuff:* Cuff measures 8⅜" × 12¾". Cut piece of linen fabric slightly larger than cuff measurement. Trace design and transfer onto fabric following positioning charts (Fig. 1). Embroider (*see* **BASIC EMBROIDERY STITCHES**); press with wrong side down. Mark fold line with row of basting stitches. Stitch side seams together with design inside; press seams open. Fold up along fold line and press. Seam allowance on top will extend over bottom half after bottom half has been folded up. (See diagram 1-4.) Turn inside out so that design is on outside. Insert right side of cuff into finished boot against lining (right side of cuff with seam in center back and design in front). Insert until seam allowance of boot and lining meets seam allowance at top of cuff; stitch around. Pull cuff and fold over top of boot. Press top edges.

*Color photo on page 67*

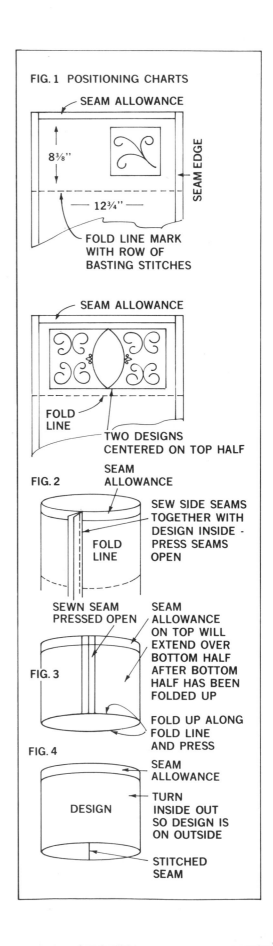

# Boxes to Fill, Trims for the Tree

**SNOWMAN COOKIE JAR**

MATERIALS: Glass jar suitable for cookies; paper for pattern; pencil; masking tape; tissue paper in assorted colors; Elmer's Glue-All®; paintbrush; Crystal Clear Krylon Spray.

DIRECTIONS: Draw a snowman or any design of your choice on paper. The pattern should be the actual size desired on the cookie jar. Tape the pattern temporarily to the inside of the jar, with the design facing out. Tear or cut the tissue paper into fingernail-sized pieces. In a cup, put three tablespoons of glue and one tablespoon of water. Mix thoroughly. With a brush, paint some of the solution on a small area on the outside of the glass jar, following the pattern design. While the glue-painted area is still moist, place a few pieces of tissue on the moist area. Brush a little of the glue mixture over the tissue pieces. repeat in another area, slightly overlapping the first area. When the design area is completely covered with tissue pieces, add details cut from tissue. Give the completed design a thin brushed-on layer of the glue mixture. Allow to dry completely. When dry, give the entire outside of the jar a thin layer of Crystal Clear Krylon Spray. Let dry; repeat. Remove the taped pattern from inside the jar.

*Color photo on page 68*

## COLORFUL TISSUE WRAP

It's hard to believe all of the colorful gift boxes shown here are wrapped in solid color tissue paper. Many are "tied" with strips of contrasting tissue or with gold gift wrap that's been zigzagged, scalloped or folded. Strips are secured at the back with cellophane tape. For a festive touch we used a hole punch on the folded strips of one box and saved the cutouts to use, confetti-style, on another. Other accents are notary seals, stick-on stars and trim and free-form designs of gold cord or thread.

## DECORATED BOXES

(2½″, 4½″, and 5½″ in diameter)

MATERIALS: Re-cycled cheese boxes or round wood boxes, (available from Leewards, 1200 St. Charles Road, Elgin, Ill. 60120); pine cones, seeds, pods; scraps of ribbon; clear silicone adhesive; clear glaze.

DIRECTIONS:

1. *Make daisies:* Cut cardboard circle ¾″ to 1″ diameter for base. Coat base thickly with clear silicone adhesive. Press seeds into a flat ring around edge of base, press acorn cup in center. Make larger daisies the same way,

but add a second ring of petals inside the first. Let harden for several hours, and attach to small dry twigs.

2. Spray all trims, except ribbons, with clear glaze.

3. Fold ribbon into loops and glue or staple to box top. With silicone adhesive, attach trims to box top over ribbons.

## KITCHEN CANISTER SET

MATERIALS: 3 plastic canisters with straight sides (drum shaped); ⅓ yd. duck-like printed cotton fabric; 1 package jumbo rickrack; 1 package baby rickrack; Scotch Spra-Ment® adhesive; Scotch Super Strength® adhesive; scissors.

DIRECTIONS: Measure the circumference and the height of each canister. Cut fabric so that its dimensions match the canister's height exactly and allow for a ½″ overlap around the circumference of each canister. Apply Scotch Spra-Ment® to the wrong side of each fabric piece and adhere fabric to canisters, carefully aligning top and bottom edges. Using Scotch Super Strength® adhesive sparingly, glue a strip of baby rickrack to the top and bottom of each canister, covering the raw edges of fabric. Trim lids of canisters with fabric and jumbo rickrack as desired. Use Scotch Spra-Ment® adhesive to adhere fabric and Scotch Super Strength® adhesive to glue jumbo rickrack to canister lids.

## PHELT®-COVERED BOXES

MATERIALS: Phun Phelt® (available from

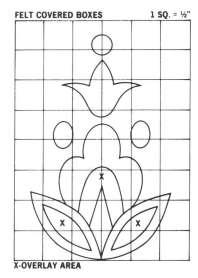

FELT COVERED BOXES          1 SQ. = ½″

X-OVERLAY AREA

the Pellon Corp., 1120 Ave. of the Americas, N.Y., N.Y. 10036), in various amounts and colors (varies with size of box); craft glue; gift boxes or similar type cardboard boxes with loose-fitting lids; white paint (spray or brush-on) if boxes are not white; pencil; scissors; ruler; tracing paper; pinking shears (for scalloping edges).

DIRECTIONS: Remove lid from box. If box is not white, paint outside white. Dry well. Cover lid and bottom, inside and out, with Phelt®. *To cover outside:* Place Phelt® on a flat surface. Place box (or lid) on it and cut Phelt® so that a sufficient amount extends on all sides to cover the sides plus about 1″ extra. For lid, have enough extra to extend up the inside of lid. Glue box in exact center of Phelt® cut to above instructions. Bring Phelt® up on sides of two opposite ends of box or lid. Glue. Cut according to diagram, allowing small tab to fit around on uncovered sides. Glue these tabs in place. Bring up remaining Phelt® and trim off what extends beyond corners of box or lid. Glue. Bring excess to inside and glue. *To line lid:* The excess from outside will finish sides, so simply cut a piece of Phelt® to fit inside of top and glue in place. Trim with scalloped bands of contrasting color, if desired. *To line bottom:* Cut pieces of Phelt® to fit all inside areas and glue in place. *To trim boxes:* Following directions on page 140, enlarge and trace design on paper. Cut out and use as pattern to cut Phelt®. Assemble in a pleasing pattern on lid. Glue in place. Add strips of scallop-edged Phelt® to accent design.

## HEART TREE ORNAMENTS

MATERIALS: Scraps of solid red fabric; scraps of red print fabric; red thread; polyester stuffing; black thread for hanging; scissors; pencil; paper for pattern.

DIRECTIONS: Following directions on page 140, enlarge heart designs, page 82, onto paper; cut out. Small ornaments are made with size 1 and size 2 hearts, larger ornaments with sizes 1, 2 and 3 hearts. Using patterns, cut out required heart sizes from fabric. Center size 1 heart on size 2 heart and appliqué with zigzag stitch. For larger ornament, center this on size 3 heart and zigzag. With right sides facing, stitch two hearts together around edge, leaving opening on one side. Turn right side out; stuff. Slipstitch closed. Stitch thread loop for hanging.

## GILDED BOX

MATERIALS: Wooden box; spray primer; polyurethane spray varnish; nonmetallic liquid solder (¾ oz. tubes), 4 for box; gold and silver leafing paint, one 1-oz. bottle of each; fine and medium sandpaper; carbon paper; very soft artists' brushes, one fine, one medium; hardware for boxes (available in hardware stores). *Optional:* Decorative lining paper; white glue.

GENERAL DIRECTIONS: *Preparing the Wood:* With primer, spray all surfaces to be decorated; let dry. Smooth with medium sandpaper; brush off dust. Repeat process five times, *or* until surface no longer becomes rough when sprayed. Use fine sandpaper for final sanding.

*Transferring Patterns:* Use carbon paper to trace enlarged patterns onto surfaces to be decorated.

*Embossing the Designs:* Make a pin hole, as small as possible, in the nozzle of the solder tube. Draw the solder along the design lines, exerting firm, uniform pressure on the tube and holding it as a felt-tip pen. Let solder dry thoroughly before adding each coat to build up the desired height; take care to apply each coat directly on previous coat.

*Painting:* Where the design is comparatively flat or shallow, paint the background area first; use a medium-wide brush and one coat of silver paint. Then paint the raised design, including the sides, with two coats of gold paint and a fine brush. Reverse the order of painting if the design is in high relief.

*Finishing:* Spray entire painted area with polyurethane varnish; let dry. Attach hardware to box. *Optional:* Glue decorative *lining paper* to box sides, bottom and top surfaces.

**Scroll-design Box** (11″×14¼″×3¾″ high): Following directions on page 140, enlarge and trace the designs on box top, sides, front and back. Use at least four coats of solder on the entire design.

1 SQ. = 1″

TOP

SIDE

FRONT AND BACK

*Color photo on page 68*

## WRAP YOUR GIFTS IN SPARKLE

Here's a way to double a gift—make the box you give it in a treasure in itself. Permanently encrusted with twinkling sequins, the box may outlive the gift! Take any cardboard or wood box, draw a simple design on it (use a compass or ruler so it will look tidy), and then, using white glue and a toothpick, fill in the design with sequins, one color at a time. Start with the pattern you've drawn on the box lid. When you've completed decorating your box, let the glue set overnight and then brush on several coats of clear polyurethane, letting dry thoroughly between each coat.

## BLACK AND SILVER DELIGHTS

For sophisticated adults, we have gift-wrap delights: A black-and-white angel design, silver foil and black-and-silver patchwork papers are adorned with small mirrors, cut-out paper appliqués, cotton clouds and stick-on black-and-silver snowflakes for a 3-D effect. Garlands of silver tinsel, strings of silver beads, Christmas balls and aluminum cooky cutters are other additions in keeping with this black-and-silver theme.

## ART DECO BOXES

MATERIALS: Assorted small tins (we used aspirin, candy and Sucrets® tins); Krylon Bright Silver Enamel Spray; ¾" and 1¼"-wide paper ribbon in assorted colors; razor-blade or X-acto® knife; scissors; double-sided clear tape (preferably with peel-off liner; if that is not available, use freezer paper as a backing); tracing paper; pencil.

DIRECTIONS: Spray tins with at least two coats of silver enamel, let each coat dry thoroughly. Draw designs on liner of tape with ribbon stuck to other side. If tape has no liner, set a section of the tape (larger than ribbon piece) down on the waxy side of freezer paper. Adhere ribbon to tape and cut freezer paper down to size. Draw designs on freezer paper. Use photo as guide. Cut out, and remove backing piece by piece as you assemble design on the tin. Smooth down securely by placing a piece of tracing paper over the design and pushing down with your thumb.

## YARN TASSEL ORNAMENT

MATERIALS: 4-ply knitting worsted (wool or synthetic) in various colors; scraps of colored felt; small pieces of stiff cardboard (see directions); scissors; ruler; white glue; thread.

DIRECTIONS: *Star:* Cut cardboard 4¼"×3". Wrap yarn (any color) 60 times around the 4¼" length. Slip cardboard out carefully and tie yarn tightly at center. Do *not* cut ends of yarn tassel. Fan ends out to make a flat circle. Divide into five equal portions and tie each portion about ¾" from outer end. Cut star shape about 2" high from white felt. Cut a slightly smaller star from a contrasting color felt. Glue the smaller star to the larger and glue to yarn tassel star shape. Cut five tiny dots from felt and glue to each point on the star. Attach thread loop for hanging.

## HEIRLOOM TREE ORNAMENTS

With a little imagination, you can turn out lovely ornaments that you'll treasure for years. You start with ordinary silver glass balls and come up with a beautiful design. Simply glue on bits of velvet, patterned, grosgrain or embroidered ribbons with lots of bows and lace ruffles, stiffened with spray starch. We used antique decals, but cutouts from old Christmas cards or gift wrap will also work. If you use figures cut from paper, glue them onto a lightweight cardboard backing to give them body. Spray-on varnishes for paper also add sheen.

*Color photo on page 70*

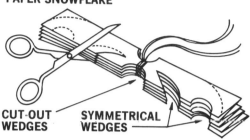

OPTIONAL NOTCHES FOR PAPER SNOWFLAKE

CUT-OUT WEDGES    SYMMETRICAL WEDGES

## PAPER SNOWFLAKES

MATERIALS: White typing paper (you can make two ornaments per 8½"×11" sheet); white glue; heavy-duty white thread; sharp scissors.

DIRECTIONS:
1. Cut paper in half lengthwise.
2. Fold crosswise into ½" accordion pleats.
3. Cut away a wedge of paper from each long side at center (*see illustration*).
4. Cut 24" of thread and double it. Tie around paper at notch to secure pleating (*see illustration*).
5. Cut out symmetrical wedges each side of the first ones, varying the number of cutouts and the shapes you cut to create as many snowflake designs as Mother Nature.
6. Run a line of white glue along one outside pleat of paper. Place thread-ends on glue strip. Open the pleating and sandwich threads with the opposite outside pleat. Now open and glue together other sides of pleating to complete snowflake.
7. Knot thread-ends and use as tree hanger.

## RIBBON-TRIMMED EGGS

To accomplish these timeless designs, paint eggshells a solid color, or rub with iridescent metallic wax for an antique patina. When completely dry, dress up in patchwork style with glued-on rows of lace, delicate floral embroidered ribbons, velvet or embroidery floss.

*Color photo on page 68*

## FOIL-COVERED ORNAMENTS

MATERIALS: Posterboard or thin shirt cardboard; foil gift wrap in assorted colors; rubber cement; thread; paper for patterns; pencil; carbon paper; scissors; straight pin.
DIRECTIONS: Enlarge patterns, following directions on page 140, and draw full-size designs on paper. Using carbon paper, transfer pattern designs onto shirt cardboard or posterboard; cut out cardboard pieces. (Do

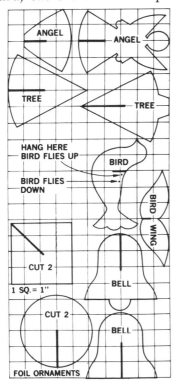

not cut slits yet.) As on cardboard, transfer pattern designs to paper side of foil wrap; cut foil pieces slightly larger than pattern outlines. (For each cardboard piece cut, you must cut 2 foil pieces.) Coat foil pieces with rubber cement on paper sides. Place cardboard piece on cemented area and smooth down firmly. Allow to dry. Cut away excess foil. Repeat on opposite side of cardboard piece. Place pattern over foil-covered shape and mark the slit (slight pressure with a pencil tip will do it). Cut slit with scissors in a smooth, even stroke. Punch hole for hanger. Knot to make loop. Slide foil pieces together in appropriate slots. (On birds, you may wish to bend wings back slightly.)

## CALICO-POTPOURRI ORNAMENTS

MATERIALS:
1. Potpourri. You can find potpourri in many gift and department stores, or you may wish to make your own (*see recipe*). The amount you make or buy will depend on how many ornaments you wish to make. One ounce or so should make 10 to 15 ornaments (allowing a small teaspoon potpourri for each ornament).
2. Assorted calico prints (or any scraps of

cotton fabric from your sewing chest). Use closely woven cotton, so the potpourri filling does not come through the fabric. Allow ¼ yard per ornament.

3. Cardboard patterns for ornaments, approximately 3″×3″.

4. Pinking shears.

DIRECTIONS:

1. Cut out cardboard patterns for ornaments. Any simple geometric shape will do—circles, stars, and squares are the easiest to sew and fill.

2. Lay pattern on fabric, with wrong side of fabric facing up. Trace around pattern outline with a pen or pencil. Cut out fabric shapes with pinking shears so the edges of the fabric will not fray. Cut two identical shapes for each ornament you intend to make. You may wish to use two fabric designs for each ornament, with a different print on each side.

3. Using pinking shears, cut out strips of fabric 4″ long and 1″ wide for hanging loops. Fold each strip in half lengthwise and press with iron.

4. Place two identical fabric shapes together, wrong sides facing, and sew by machine or hand approximately ¾ of the way around the edge, making the seam about ⅜″ in from edge. Leave an opening for inserting potpourri.

5. Pour approximately one small teaspoon of potpourri inside each partially sewn ornament. Make a loop with a folded fabric strip and insert ends of loop into opening and finish sewing up the opening.

## CHRISTMAS POTPOURRI

To 1 quart of fir needles, add:
  1 cup dried mixed citrus peels*
    (grapefruit, lemon, orange, lime),
    coarsely broken (whirl in blender)
  1 cup whole rosemary
  ½ cup dried whole basil
  2 to 4 whole bay leaves, coarsely crumbled
  2 cups coarse (not iodized) salt**

Mix all ingredients together and use to stuff fabric tree ornaments. Warmth brings out the fragrance. If fir needles are not obtainable, the potpourri will be deliciously fragrant in any case!

*To prepare citrus peels, remove membrane, cut into strips, dry in a warm place till very crisp and brittle. Break into small pieces and store in plastic bags tightly sealed.

**Coarse (kosher-type) salt is a fixative to help hold fragrance.

## POINSETTIA BALLS

MATERIALS: White bread; white glue; food coloring; pastry tube; seed pearls; silver ornaments.

DIRECTIONS: Tear up white bread and mix it with white glue. Tint some of the mixture with red food coloring. Put in pastry tube and squeeze carefully onto silver balls in flower shapes as shown in photo. Press seed pearls in centers of flowers. Let dry.

to dry before adding the next. Small curls on tree ornaments were rolled around the stem of a cotton swab.

## ORGANDY ROSE BUD BOUQUETS
Following the directions on page 20 make as many rose buds as your tree will gracefully hold. Tie them in bouquets with baby's breath and velvet ribbons and attach them to your tree.

## BROWN PAPER ORNAMENTS
MATERIALS: Brown paper bags; white glue; scissors; pencil.
DIRECTIONS: All ornaments are made from 1½" to 2"-wide strips cut from paper bag. Each strip is cut to desired length, then folded lengthwise into thirds. It is unfolded, spread inside with glue, then refolded and glued into thirds. For all ornaments shown, simply glue strips, rolled or bent in the appropriate ways while still wet, following photograph for basic construction. To roll strips for curls and curves, wind strip (while glue is still wet) around a pencil or other round object. Tight winding will produce small curls, loose winding larger curls. Let curls dry on pencil, then slip them off. Allow each section

## RAINBOW REINDEER
MATERIALS: One 8"×10" piece of felt in each of the following colors: red, orange, yellow, green, blue, purple and white; polyester fiberfill; heavy cotton thread; white glue.
DIRECTIONS: Following directions on page 140, enlarge and trace reindeer and antler shapes onto paper. Fold each felt piece (except white) in half. Place pattern for reindeer body on folded felt and cut two reindeer body pieces. Repeat for all six colors. For antlers, fold white felt in half, place antler pattern on

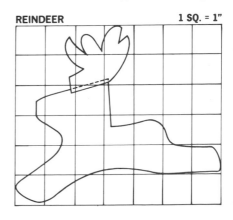

REINDEER     1 SQ. = 1"

jacket trim (see photo). For hat, cut 2" circle from a paper plate. Cut a slit from edge of circle to center. Wind into cone shape until it fits over top of clothespin; glue closed (but do not glue to clothespin); let dry. Trim off any excess paper. Wind and glue gold cord around cone until it is completely covered. Fit hat over top of clothespin and glue in place. For tassel, cut another piece of paper plate or cardboard into a 2" square. Wind crochet cotton around cardboard about 60 times. Thread piece of cotton under strands at top of cardboard and tie strands together, knotting firmly and leaving long ends to use, tying onto top of gold cone. Cut strands open at bottom of cardboard. Tie strands together 1/3 of the way down from tied-off top. Attach to hat with long ends left for this purpose. Trim waist and side of "pants" with gold cord glued in place (see photo).

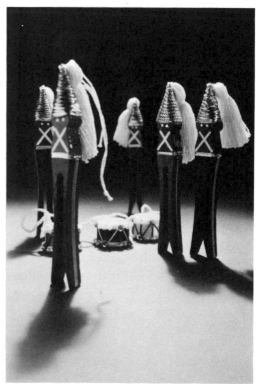

*Color photo on page 69*

top, and cut out 6 double pieces (12 altogether). Sew pairs of reindeer body pieces together, leaving an opening at the head. Stuff lightly and evenly with polyester fiberfill. Glue sets of antlers together, *except* for part that fits over reindeer's head. Slightly overlap this part on the head. Hand sew antlers onto head (this also closes reindeer body opening). Cut six 8" lengths of cotton thread. With large needle, attach one to each reindeer directly behind the antlers. Knot and hang.

## CLOTHESPIN SOLDIERS AND DRUMS
### SOLDIERS
MATERIALS: Wooden one-piece clothespins; narrow gold cord; scissors; uncoated paper plate; pencil; white glue; paint brush; enamel paint (white, red, blue, black); white crochet cotton.

DIRECTIONS: Paint bottom of clothespin black or blue (for legs); paint top red or white; let dry. (Use several coats for a high glossy finish.) Add white dots for eyes and "X" for

### DRUMS
MATERIALS: Spools of silk thread (red, white and blue); crochet cotton (same as for tassels on soldiers); white glue; sequins, beads and pearls.

DIRECTIONS: Remove 1 round of silk from each spool. Use silk (doubled) to make crisscross design. Glue thread on carefully, making sure not to get any glue on the silk as it will spot. Cover top and bottom of spool with crochet cotton, gluing on in spiral fashion. Braid white cotton to make hanger. Glue onto spool and cover these ends with sequins and beads. Cover top and bottom edges of spool with pearls.

## CLOTHESPIN DOLLS

MATERIALS: Wooden clothespin for each doll; white pipe cleaner for each doll; 3"-wide ruffled eyelet (each long skirt takes about 3"); 1"-wide double-edged ruffled eyelet (each ballerina takes about 6"); ¾"-wide hearts and flowers patterned braid (each peasant takes about 8", each ballerina about 2½"); 1"-wide beading (each long-sleeved blouse takes about 8", each shawl for Victorian Lady about 4"); narrow ribbon to thread through beading and for bows (each front bow takes about 8", each head bow takes about 3"); 2" daisies (one per angel) from daisy braid; 1"-diameter lace daisies for hats; colored nosegays from braid

for bouquets and hats; beading edged with ¾"-wide ruffled eyelet (each angel takes about 2½"); 1"-wide velvet ribbon (each Victorian shawl takes about 4"); scraps of lace (or substitute your own scraps of ribbon, lace, eyelet, braid for much of the above); fine-tipped felt markers; fabric glue.

DIRECTIONS:

1. Paint hair and eyes on each clothespin "head" with felt-tip marker.

2. Wind a pipe cleaner securely around each doll about ¼" down from neck, leaving a 2" end on either side for arms. Glue in place.

3. *Ballerina:* Wind braid around doll's chest, cutting tiny armholes for arms to slip through, and glue securely at back, overlapping ends. Sew together ends of double-edged eyelet and run a row of gathering stitches along center. Slip onto each doll, draw gathers tightly around doll's waist and glue in place. Glue a small medallion from lacy braid or heavy lace to back of head for headdress.

4. *Angel:* Wind 3"-wide eyelet ruffle around doll below arms, glue in place, and glue or sew together overlapping edges at back. Wind ruffled beading around chest, slipping arms through ribbon slots. Glue overlapping ends together at back. Turn upper ruffle down to form wide collar. Glue a 2" daisy to back to form halo/wings. Glue a nosegay into hands.

5. *Victorian Dolls:* Attach skirt as for Angel. For an *Eliza Doolittle doll,* wrap velvet ribbon around shoulders for "shawl", gluing overlap in front. Glue violet nosegay into hands and a 1" daisy to back of head. For *Victorian lady,* wrap 1" beading, threaded with narrow ribbon, across front of shoulders and glue in a V at back. Sew ribbon bow with long ends in front. Glue nosegay to one hand.

6. *Peasant:* Attach skirt as for Angel. Glue a lace medallion in front for "apron." Spread doll's arms straight out from body and wrap braid along full arms' reach, gluing ends in back to form "blouse." Make holes in braid to slip hands through. Sew side seams through braid and stitch edges together at shoulders to hold blouse in place. Glue ribbon bow to head.

7. Other dolls with long-sleeved blouses are made same as peasant with lace-threaded beading instead of braid for blouse. Use nosegays for hats and bouquets.

## LITTLE SILVER PAILS

MATERIALS: Juice cans (6 fluid ounce size); silver spray paint (available at the 5&10); silver tinsel cord; small saw or knife; Sobo or other white glue.

DIRECTIONS: With small saw or knife, cut each can 1¾" from bottom. Spray with silver paint, following directions on can. Let dry. Glue cord around top edge and just above rim of bottom edge. For handle, cut cord 9" long and tie a knot ½" from each end. Unravel ends into fringe. Glue knots to basket ½" below top edge and glue handle to cord around top edge where they touch.

## ROSEBUD CHRISTMAS TREE ORNAMENTS

GENERAL MATERIALS: The rose-embroidered appliqués used on our ornaments are sold individually or by the yard in fabric trim departments. Fabric cutouts would be a practical substitute. All ornaments require white glue, scissors, pencil and pins.

ROSEBUD BALLS

MATERIALS (for one ball): One white satin-covered ball, 3" in diameter; two deep rose appliqués, 3" long; 1½ yds. gold soutache braid; ½"-wide green, woven-edge velvet ribbon, ⅓ yd.

DIRECTIONS: Using pencil line, divide ball into halves from hanging loop. Glue ribbon around ball on line, using pins to fasten until glue is dry. Glue two rows of soutache on each side of the ribbon. Glue rose appliqué to each side of ball. Make bow of soutache and glue to top of ball.

ROSEBUD BELLS

MATERIALS (for one bell): One satin-covered bell, 3" long; four pale rose appliqués; ½"-wide dusty rose, woven-edge velvet ribbon, ¼ yd.; ½ yd. soutache braid.

DIRECTIONS: Glue velvet ribbon as a band around the widest part of the bell. Use pins to hold ribbon until dry. Glue soutache on each side of ribbon. Glue four rose appliqués equally spaced around the bell.

DIAMOND-SHAPED ORNAMENTS

MATERIALS (for one ornament): ½"-wide old rose ribbon with picot edge, ½ yd.; ⅜"-wide lace with a scalloped edge, 14"; ¼"-wide gold middy braid, 1 yd.; gold soutache braid, 3"; one white tassel, 1½" long; six-strand embroidery floss: Scraps of dark green, medium green, deep pink and pale pink; 16 holes-to-the-inch perforated embroidery paper, one sheet. (Available at PURSEnalities, a division of Sew Industries Inc., 1619 Grand Ave., Baldwin, N.Y. 11510)

DIRECTIONS: First stitch a 2¾" long-stemmed rose with a 1"-long flower, working on the diagonal in the center of a 3" square of perforated paper, using the close-up photo on page 69 as a guide for placement. Use the Cross Stitch (see BASIC EMBROIDERY STITCHES) for the flower, with two strands of floss doubled to make four strands. The pink border surrounding the flower is worked with a Half Cross Stitch (see BASIC NEEDLEPOINT STITCHES) with three strands of floss doubled to make six strands. Work stitches straight up and down through

*Color photo on page 69*

paper, being careful not to pull stitches too tightly. When completed, trim paper two holes beyond border. *To assemble:* Glue picot edge ribbon to one side of cardboard square with ribbon extending just beyond edge of cardboard. Glue lace inside and overlapping ribbon square. Center and glue embroidered perforated paper inside of square. Glue middy braid to cover paper edge and inner edge of lace. Glue felt to reverse side of ornament. Glue middy braid around edge on back. Glue loop of soutache to top of ornament and tassel to opposite point.

## ANGELS AND CLOUDS MOBILE

MATERIALS: Three-ply bristol board or any other paper of medium to heavy weight with a slight texture; scissors or mat knife; nylon tip markers in royal blue, light blue, gold, light orange, rose and light gray; embroidery needle; heavyweight black cotton thread; three ¼" dowels, each 6" long.

DIRECTIONS: *For Making Angels and Clouds:* Following directions on page 140, enlarge the patterns for angels with trumpets, angels with stars and clouds. Cut out the enlarged patterns and then cut out 2 angels with trumpets, 3 angels with stars and 2 clouds. Color all pieces with markers, making clouds and hair yellow, stars gold, belts light and royal blue and trumpets royal blue. Using embroidery needle, poke a hole in each piece for hanging with thread.

DIRECTIONS: *For Hanging:* Knot a long piece of the heavy black thread at the center of one dowel. Loop the free end of the thread and hang this from a ceiling fixture or any other device that will allow the mobile to hang so that it does not touch anything. At one end of this first dowel, hang an angel with a trumpet from a thread 3¼" long. At the other end, hang an angel with a star from a thread 1¾" long. In the center, tie on another thread, 7" long and attach thread to the center of the second dowel. On this second dowel, hang an angel with a trumpet, a cloud and an angel with a star on threads 1½", 3¼", 5½", respectively. Hang the third dowel another 7" down from the second, maintaining a good balance and adding the remaining angel and cloud on threads about 3" and 1". Vary the positions to get a pleasing and balanced composition and then tighten all knots.

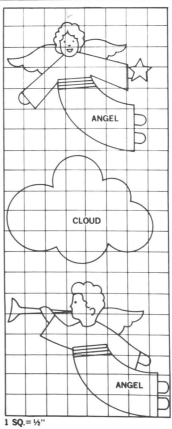

1 SQ. = ½"

## HEARTS AND FLOWERS

MATERIALS: Tracing paper; shirt cardboard; white glue; leftover pieces of yarn such as knitting worsted; pair of small scissors; orange stick or similar implement; thread.

DIRECTIONS: Trace flower and heart patterns; transfer to cardboard; cut out. Apply glue in sections (a little at a time), starting from outside edges and working toward center. After gluing edges, press yarn onto surface. Glue area next to yarn and apply more yarn. Continue this procedure until one side is completed, cutting yarn whenever you want to change colors. When one side is completed, leave to dry between telephone books. Work other side the same way after first gluing length of thread to cardboard for hanging ornament.

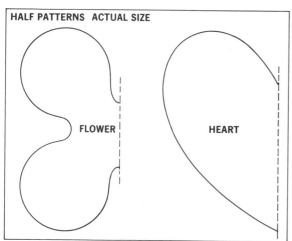

HALF PATTERNS ACTUAL SIZE

FLOWER

HEART

TISSUE AND PLASTIC ORNAMENTS

1 SQ. = 1"

## TISSUE-AND-PLASTIC ORNAMENTS

MATERIALS: Clear, thin plastic sheet (easy to cut with a scissors); tissue paper in assorted colors; black permanent felt-tipped marker; scissors; Elmer's Glue-All®; narrow paintbrush; paper; thread.

DIRECTIONS: Following directions on page 140, enlarge designs on paper. Place plastic sheet over designs and trace with felt-tipped marker. Carefully cut out the plastic designs. Cut or tear the tissue paper into fingernail-sized pieces. Brush a small amount of glue on a small area of plastic. Place a piece of tissue on the moist glue, and then brush a thin coat of glue over the tissue. Place more tissue pieces down, overlapping as you go. Only cover one side of the plastic. When the entire side has been covered with the colored pieces of tissue, coat the entire side with glue. Trim off any excess tissue that may extend beyond the edge. Allow to dry thoroughly. Details and outlines may be added with a permanent felt-tipped marker. Pierce a hole at the top and hang with thread.

## GERANIUM CASCADE TRIMS

MATERIALS: Red velvet for petals (from ¼ yd. you can make about 10 cascades of seven flowers each); 3″-wide green satin floral ribbon for leaves (1 yd. makes about 48 leaves); #26 wire, red-covered for petals and green-covered for leaves; #30 or #32 fine gold wire; small gold beads; clear acrylic spray; white glue; fine-line green felt-tip pen; green floral tape; wire clippers.

DIRECTIONS:
1. Spray the wrong side of velvet and of floral ribbon with a light coat of acrylic. Let dry and spray again.
2. Trace the actual-size leaf and petal patterns onto thin cardboard.
3. *Petals:* Trace five velvet petals for each flower; cut out. Cut #26 red wire into pieces 2″ to 3″ long. With white glue, attach a wire to the back of each petal and let dry (each cascade is made up of five small and two large flowers).
4. *Stamens:* Cut fine gold wire into pieces 5″ long. Thread each piece through a gold bead and twist the ends together tightly.
5. *Flowers:* Twist together the stems of five petals and one stamen (three stamens for the larger flowers). Wrap stem with floral tape.
6. *Leaves:* Cut five leaves for each cascade. Cut green covered wire into 2″–3″ pieces. With white glue, attach a wire to the back of

*Color photo on page 69*

each leaf and let dry. Make leaf markings with green pen.

7. *Cascades:* Cut one piece of #26 green wire about 6″ long for base of cascade. With floral tape wrap two small flowers and two leaves to one end of the wire. Continue wrapping and, about 1½″ away, tape three more small flowers and one leaf. At the top end of the base wire, tape two large flowers and two leaves. (While taping you may wish to trim some stem wires to make a closer cluster.) Bend wires at the top end into a hook which can hang from a tree or package.

## COVERED STYROFOAM BALLS

MATERIALS (for 10 large balls): 2″, 3″ or 4″ diameter styrofoam balls, 10; 45″-wide fabric (we used satin pin dot and plain and check synthetic taffeta), 1 yd. for 4″ balls, ¾ yd. for 3″ balls and ½ yd. for 2″ balls; ½″-wide ribbon to wrap balls, 10 yds. for 4″ balls, 7½ yds. for 3″ balls, 6½ yds. for 2″ balls; 1¼″-wide ribbon for bows, 5 yds.; 60 flowers and 40 leaves (*see* GERANIUM CASCADE TRIMS) for 3″ and 4″ balls; 30 flowers and 30 leaves for 2″ balls; 10 fern or T-pins; 10 ornament hangers; straight pins.

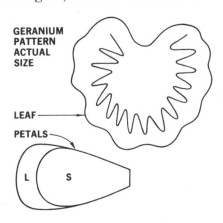

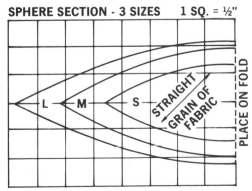

DIRECTIONS:

1. Following the directions on page 140, enlarge the sphere sections and cut out separate patterns for each size; add grain arrows. Placing the arrow along a straight grain, trace around patterns on fabric. Cut eight sections for each ball.

2. Pin tips of one section to the ball, then pin the section opposite. Pin remaining sections to ball, overlapping edges and tips until ball is covered.

3. Wrap narrow ribbon around ball, covering the intersecting tips of fabric. Overlap and trim the ribbon ends, and pin them to ball. Repeat, to wrap another ribbon at right angles to the first.

4. With floral tape, wrap three geraniums and two leaves to make a spray (see directions for GERANIUM CASCADE TRIMS. Make a second spray. Pin them to top of ball, trimming stems as necessary.

5. Tie ½ yd. of ribbon in a bow and pin to top of ball.

6. Insert fern or T-pin in top of ball and attach an ornament hanger to it.

## FABRIC TREE DECORATIONS

MATERIALS (for each ornament): Various colors of medium-weight, firmly woven fabric, scraps for the small appliqués, and larger pieces for the ornament face and back; lightweight cardboard; large spools colored thread; wrapping paper; dressmaker's carbon; tracing wheel; tapestry needle; red yarn, about 24″.

DIRECTIONS:

1. Following the directions on page 140, enlarge and cut out the ornament patterns.

2. Using dressmaker's carbon, trace the outline of the star and heart patterns onto cardboard and two fabrics; cut out. Trace the other patterns onto 3½″ circles cut from cardboard and two fabrics. Trim ⅛″ from edges of all cardboard pieces.

3. To make the appliqués, trace the individual pattern sections (leaves, flowers, bird's wings, etc.) onto fabric scraps; cut out. Pin, then baste, the appliqué sections in place within the traced outlines on the fabric circle.

1 SQ.=1″

With contrasting thread and a tight machine satin stitch, slightly narrower than ⅛", stitch around all edges of each appliqué piece.

4. With the cardboard between, pin the appliquéd circles to the backing circles; pin the fabric star and hearts together. Satin stitch, twice around the fabric edges.

5. Use a large eye needle to pull yarn through the center top edge of the ornament; knot the yarn, leaving the ends of even length.

## CHRISTMAS ANGEL

MATERIALS: Pale pink cotton, ⅜ yds.; white polished cotton, ½ yd.; *eyelet ruffling* in the following widths and yardage: 5"-wide, 2½ yds., 2"-wide ½ yd., 1"-wide 1½ yd.; white organdy ¼ yd.; dotted Swiss 12" × 12"; ¼"-wide white rickrack, 1 package; *satin ribbons in following widths and yardage:* 3/16"-wide 2 yds., ½"-wide 1½ yd., ⅞"-wide ½ yd.; gold decorative braid 2¾ yds.; *embroidery floss* in the following colors: Light pink, dark pink, medium blue, soft brown, white; two gold-colored pot scrubbers; 5"-length cut from cardboard paper toweling tube; flexible copper or florist wire, about 4'; fabric glue; polyester fiberfill; dressmaker's carbon and tracing wheel; ice cream stick; 5" embroidery hoop.

DIRECTIONS: Following directions on page 140, enlarge and cut out the angel pattern pieces. Using enlarged patterns, cut from pink fabric two body pieces, four hand pieces and one head piece; on a 6" square of pink fabric, *trace* the head pattern including the facial features; this piece will be cut out *after embroidering* the features. From white organdy, cut one 12" × 28" piece for underskirt. From polished cotton, cut two sleeves, one 13" × 29" piece for overskirt and two 2" × 5½" strips for shoulder bands. Seam allowance is ½" on clothes and ¼" on body parts.

1. With Satin Stitch (*see* BASIC EMBROIDERY STITCHES), embroider facial features on traced head piece, using photo as guide. Cut out head on marked outline.

2. With right sides together, seam head front to back, and hand fronts to backs, leaving an opening in top edges; seam body front to back, leaving top and bottom edges open. Trim seams; clip curves. Turn all pieces right side out. Stuff hands, head and upper part of body with polyester fill. Slipstitch openings in head and hands. Insert an ice cream stick between body stuffing and fabric, with top extending upward about 2" to be attached later to the head. Add body stuffing as needed to fill out torso.

3. Make two rows of maching-gathering stitches on top and bottom edges of sleeves and on one long edge of underskirt and over-skirt.

4. On the underskirt, turn the other long edge ¼" to *right sides*; press fold. Pin finished edge of 1" ruffling over raw edge; topstitch in place. Stitch center back seam. Gather top edge to fit around the center of the 5" tube; glue in place.

*Color photo on page 70*

1 SQ. = 1"

5. On the overskirt, make a 2″ hem on the other long edge; topstitch rickrack along the hem stitching line. Topstitch 5″ ruffling in three tiers, measuring from the skirt bottom edge as follows: 5″, 7½″ and 9″. Stitch center back seam, with the ruffle edges aligned. Gather the top edge to fit tube; glue in place, making sure the underskirt ruffle shows at bottom.

6. Stitch sleeve seams. Gather top edge to fit shoulder and bottom edge to fit wrist. Topstitch 1″ ruffling and gold braid to bottom edge. Stitch gathered edges in place on shoulder and wrists.

7. Bend wire to the shape of the wing pattern. On the right side of the dotted Swiss, glue wire wings and weight; let dry. Cut away excess fabric around wire. Glue gold braid on both sides of wings, covering the wire.

*Assembling the Angel*

1. Slip the torso over the top of the tube; glue in place.

2. Fold under ½″ on both long edges of shoulder bands; press. Lightly glue ½″ satin ribbon down center of bands, and tiny rickrack along each side of ribbon. Glue 1″ ruffling to underside of outer edge of each band. Pin bands in place on shoulders, tucking a small piece of ruffling between them in front; glue in place front and back.

3. Sew 2″ ruffling around waist as top layer of skirt. Glue 1″ satin ribbon around waist, covering all raw edges.

4. Make tiny bows from ³/₁₆″ satin ribbon; tack in place on skirt, as shown in photo. From ½″ satin ribbon, make a 2″ bow with long streamers. Tack to top ruffle on skirt back.

5. Arrange the head on the neck at the correct height. Glue Popsicle stick to back of head; whipstitch neck to head securely. Arrange pot scrubbers to look like hair; tack to head in several places. Arrange some tendrils in a curly effect around face, and in a topknot, with a narrow ribbon tied in a bow around it.

6. Sew the center of the wings securely to the waistline in back.

## DOVES

MATERIALS: White fabric, such as fine nylon jersey or tricot; white thread; polyester fiberfill for stuffing; beads or silver sequins for eyes; crochet cotton or thread for hanging; dowel about 11″ long.

DIRECTIONS: Following directions on page 140, enlarge pattern. Use pattern to cut 10 pieces from white fabric—2 for each dove. (If fabric has a right and wrong side, remember to turn pattern over for a left and right side of bird.) Stitch the 2 sides of bird together, wrong sides facing, using zigzag stitch close to the edge, or join by hand with a buttonhole stitch, leaving 1½″ opening at the bottom of the bird. Fill bird firmly with polyester fiberfill. Hand-stitch opening closed; sew on eyes. Cut three 7″ lengths and two 10″ lengths of crochet cotton or thread. Attach birds to thread allowing the center one and the two end birds to hang 5½″ down from dowel (see photograph for placement). Hang the remaining two birds 8½″ from dowel. Measure and attach a 1 yard length of thread to center of dowel for hanging the mobile.

DOVE

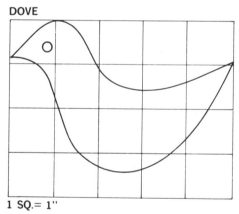

1 SQ.= 1″

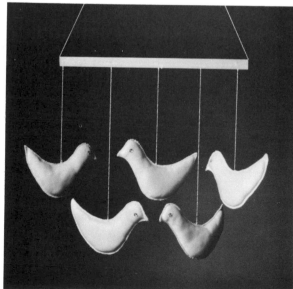

## EMBROIDERED FELT ORNAMENTS

MATERIALS: Felt or fabric remnants; embroidery floss; embroidery needle; cardboard or paper; pencil; small embroidery hoop; polyester fiberfill leftover yarn from other projects for stuffing.

DIRECTIONS: Enlarge the patterns onto paper, following directions on page 140. Trace shape onto fabric remnant that is large enough to fit into your embroidery hoop. Retrace onto a second remnant (can be a different fabric). Stay stitch around pencil line on both pieces. Embroider one or both sides as you wish, using stitches indicated in diagram. Remove from hoop and trim each piece ¼" from stay stitching. Sew right side to right, leaving opening to stuff. Clip around curves (edges) and trim closer to stay stitching. Turn right sides out; stuff. Slipstitch closed. Trim edges with Buttonhole or Blanket Stitch (*See* BASIC EMBROIDERY STITCHES) worked with floss in one direction all around. Work a second row in second color in opposite direction and in between first row. Follow diagrams for inside stitches. Use embroidery floss to make loop for hanging at top centers of ornaments.

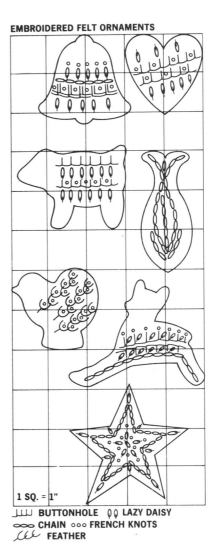

EMBROIDERED FELT ORNAMENTS

1 SQ. = 1"

⎿⎺⎽ BUTTONHOLE  ◊◊ LAZY DAISY
∞∞ CHAIN  ∘∘∘ FRENCH KNOTS
ℓℓℓ FEATHER

## COOKIE CUTTER ORNAMENTS

MATERIALS: 12 oz. tin soda or beer cans (one can makes four ornaments); white glue; hobby enamel paints; paint brush; transparent tape; can opener; utility knife; heavy-duty scissors or tin snips; metal straight edge; emery paper; drill or metal punch; thread or monofilm line.

DIRECTIONS: Using can opener, cut top and bottom from can. Cut can lengthwise at seam. Trim edges of cut can and lay flat. With utility knife and straight edge, cut 1"-wide strips approximately 7" long. Using caution, remove sharp edges from strips with emery paper. Bend and form shapes by hand. To bend a straight line, bend strip over a straight-edged object. Glue strips to one another until complete form is made. Drill a small hole for thread or monofilm line to hang completed ornament. Using transparent

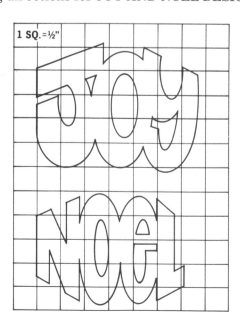

tape, mask off areas for stripes, painting several stripes in one color; allow to dry, remove tape. Re-tape other areas, paint and dry. Repeat this process until ornament is completed.

## CHRISTMAS VILLAGE DECORATIONS

MATERIALS: Styrofoam board, $^3/_{16}$"-¼" thick; white glue, mat knife or razor; nylon-tip markers; thread or lightweight wire.

DIRECTIONS:

JOY AND NOEL DESIGNS: Following directions on page 140, enlarge patterns. Cut patterns and place on sheet of Styrofoam. Trace outlines of pattern and cut out with mat knife or razor. Color with nylon-tip markers in designs of your choice; hang ornament with thread or wire.

CHURCH AND CHRISTMAS TREE: Enlarge pattern and cut out Styrofoam following directions for JOY AND NOEL DESIGNS.

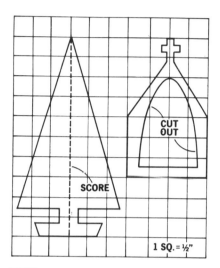

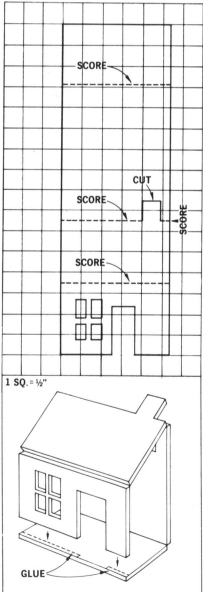

Score Christmas tree from top to base, down center. Cut another tree using same pattern and score this also. (You now have 2 parts.) Overlap pieces and glue as shown in drawing right. For church, glue cutout to frame of church to create a recessed window effect. Color both designs and attach thread or wire for hanging.

HOUSE: Enlarge pattern and cut out Styrofoam board, following directions for JOY AND NOEL DESIGNS. With mat knife, score board where indicated in drawing and cut out areas for chimney, windows and door. Color with nylon-tip markers. Glue front of house to base. Add thread or wire for hanging.

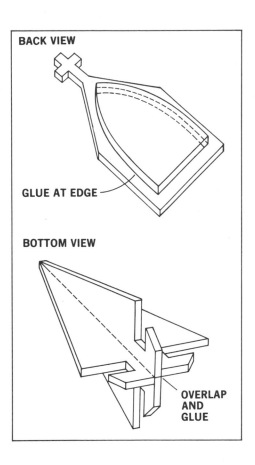

## FELT ORNAMENTS

MATERIALS: 72"-wide felt in about 10 colors, or packaged felt pieces sold in two sizes—6"×9" and 9"×12". For felt amounts required, see *Note* below. White fabric glue; brown paper and lightweight cardboard for patterns; ruler and compass; thread to match felt; large needle; green yarn (to attach felt ornaments to tree).

*Note*: How much felt to buy depends on how many items you make.

GENERAL DIRECTIONS: All of our felt decorations are quickly and easily "appliquéd" with glue. On the background felt the appliqués are built up in layers, each one glued to the one beneath and overlapped as shown in the photo. Following directions on page 140 enlarge the designs on brown wrapping paper, in the grid sizes indicated below.

*Tree-size Ornaments:* 1 sq. = ⅜".

*Cutting:*

1. Trace the full outline of each enlarged pattern onto felt. This is the background piece on which the appliqués are glued to each other in layers. Cut out.

2. Trace the background pattern and the

*Color photo on page 70*

FELT APPLIQUE DESIGNS

appliqué parts of each pattern onto the cardboard; cut out.

3. Trace patterns onto felt in appropriate colors of your choice. Cut out appliqués.
*(Note:* If your tracing lines show, use the reverse side of all pieces.)
*Gluing:*
4. Glue the appliqués in layers to the background piece, overlapping the appliqués as shown in the photo.
*Tree Ornaments:* Using needle, pull two 7″ lengths of green yarn through top of ornament. Knot ends to form a loop hanger.

## NEEDLEPOINT ORNAMENTS

MATERIALS (for 4 ornaments): 12″×12″ No. 10 mono canvas (four 6″ squares); 1 oz. red needlepoint yarn; 1 oz. green needlepoint yarn; ½ oz. white needlepoint yarn; two 4″ squares of red felt; two 4″ squares of green felt; red thread; green thread; needle; paper clips; Elmer's Glue-All®; scissors.

DIRECTIONS:
*Small Snowflake (finished size is 3¾″×3¾″):*
Measure out center of 6″ canvas square. Start with green yarn. Once you find center hole, make one stitch straight up, skipping one hole (follow top diagram). Diagonally go up one hole, stitch straight up, again skipping one hole and again go diagonally up once more. You should have 3 stitches slanting upwards. At upper left stitch, take needle in beginning hole of that stitch and go across, skipping one hole. Work your way down same way to first original stitch; bring needle up again in original hole; work 3 stitches outwards, always skipping one hole. Now stitches are slanting down. Bring needle up from bottom left-hand stitch and start working your way up to original hole. These stitches are straight up and down. Continue this until you work the pattern totally around to meet. Now switch to red yarn. Where you have 3 green stitches, continue out same way, making 3 red stitches. Where it v's in, follow around with red, also marking a "v." Continue this all the way around. Continue this same way, next using white, then green, then red, then green. Next work with red yarn. There will not be enough space for total work on this color. So where you can't skip a space, just do one upward stitch. In the four corners, use the red yarn. One stitch across, one up, and

one diagonally, all 3 stitches going into the same hole. Next use white yarn. Again, don't worry about not being able to skip a hole. However, after the 5th white stitch, do one stitch up at the bottom, not skipping a hole, then above that do another white stitch, skipping a hole. After 8 white stitches, do one green stitch, skipping a hole. Skip a space, do another green stitch, skipping a hole. Next, at bottom, do one green stitch, not skipping a hole. Above that do a green stitch, skipping a hole, next to that do another green stitch, skipping a hole. Skip one space and do a green stitch, skipping a hole. Fill in all other areas with white. You can make another ornament in the same design, but interchange green yarn and red, leaving white yarn as is.

*Large Snowflake (finished size is 4"×4")*: Measure out center of 6" canvas square. Using red yarn and starting at center hole, do 6 diagonal stitches up, skipping 2 spaces (see bottom diagram). Then do another 6 stitches, coming back to the original hole

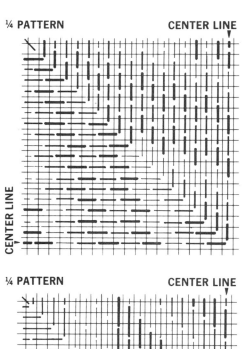

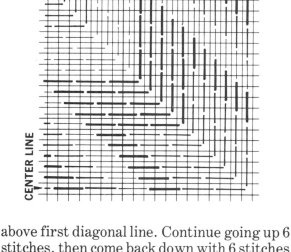

above first diagonal line. Continue going up 6 stitches, then come back down with 6 stitches underneath. You should now have a double "v" design. Now repeat this same design, with stitches going outwards. Continue around. Switch to green yarn. Starting above center of red "v," do 11 diagonal, upward stitches, skipping 2 holes. Underneath that do 5 diagonal stitches meeting red. Underneath that do 5 diagonal stitches back up, then 5 diagonal stitches outward back down (2 rows). Next, do 11 stitches, getting to center of next "v." Continue to work all the way around. Change to white. Start above center of green "v." Do 9 upward stitches, skipping 2 holes, then 1 stitch, skipping 1 hole, and 1 more stitch, not skipping a hole. Crosswise, skip 2 holes, then 1, then none, then 2. Work 2 more diagonal lines below this, then do 3 rows outwards. Continue this all the way around. Where you have 4 open "v's" on all sides, starting at center of white "v," do diagonal stitches in red (8 stitches), last 2 stitches skip 1 hole, then none, to meet with white. Do same on other side to make complete "v." Switch to green (5 stitches), then red again (3 stitches), not skipping, skipping 1, not skipping. Do this on all 4 sides. In the 4 empty corners, fill in with red, following lines of white diagonally down. To square off, put 3 stitches into same hole (across, slanted and up). Do this in all 4 corners. Make another ornament in the same design, interchanging green and red, leaving white as is.

*Finishing:* Trim edges of canvas, leaving approximately ¼″ to ½″ on all sides. Snip corners fairly close to work. With Elmer's glue, turn canvas edges back; glue. To hold them down while drying, use paper clips. Once dry, remove clips. Cut felt slightly larger than finished work and blind stitch to back in matching thread. Use tapestry yarn to make loop for hanging ornaments.

## GLASS BALL ORNAMENTS

MATERIALS: Glass ball ornaments (colored, if clear ones not available); household bleach; assorted small glass beads and pearl beads threaded on light string; shank buttons to fit opening on ornaments (or a little larger than opening); white glue; all-purpose clear water-proof glue; scissors; funnel to fit ornament opening; food coloring (optional); string or plastic fishing line for hanging; bathroom-size paper cups to use as drying stands. *Note:* Be sure that you use balls 2½″ in diameter or smaller balls if filling with water. Larger balls will be too heavy.

DIRECTIONS *To remove color from ornaments:* Remove cap from ornament; discard. Fill ornament with bleach and place in bowl or sink filled with bleach; let soak until color disintegrates, both inside and outside. (When using bleach, wear rubber gloves to protect your hands as you work.) Rinse out with running water. If any color remains, repeat process, shaking ornament gently. Rinse and let air dry thoroughly. *To decorate:* Outline patterns on ornament with line of white glue applied with toothpick or hatpin. Allow glue to set; apply strung beads. (Do not cover ornament completely with beads, but allow ample spaces for colored water to show through and to reflect light.) Cut string

and pull to remove from beads. Let dry. This will serve as outline of areas to be filled with small glass beads. Cut out bottom of paper cup to serve as holder for ornament as it is drying. Mix water with a few drops food coloring to desired color in a separate container. (Add more water if color is too dark.) With ornament sitting upright and using funnel, fill ball with colored water, being careful not to spill any on beads (they have been glued on with water-soluble glue and could wash off). Glue shank button (shank up, button front down) over opening of ornament to seal, using clear waterproof glue. Let dry thoroughly. *To hang:* Thread string or plastic fishing line through shank hole or, use thin decorative gold and silver cord for hangers.

## STAINED GLASS PENDANTS AND ORNAMENTS

GENERAL MATERIALS: Stained glass nuggets and stained or cathedral glass single lead channel (also called came); single edge razor blade; solder, 60/40; 200 watt soldering iron; felt-tipped pen; glass cutter; 20-gauge copper wire (for pear, cherries, tree).

DIRECTIONS:

FLOWER PENDANT: 6 small red nuggets;

1 small green nugget; 24″ chain.
1. Wrap single lead channel tightly around nuggets individually. Cut lead with razor blade to form a close joint on each nugget.
2. Solder joint of each nugget separately. Arrange red nuggets evenly around the green one with joints pointing toward center. Solder red nuggets to green one in center, turn pendant over and repeat these solder joinings on other side.
3. Form a ⅝″ strip of channel lead into a loop and solder to top red petal. Run chain through loop.

CROSS PENDANT: 6 small turquoise nuggets; 24″ chain.
1. Wrap single lead channel tightly around nuggets individually. Cut lead with razor blade to form a close joint on each nugget.
2. Solder joint of each nugget separately. Position 4 nuggets vertically in a straight line and solder together. Then solder two nuggets positioned horizontally, one on each side of 2nd nugget from one end; turn pendant over and repeat these solder joinings on other side.
3. Form a ⅝″ strip of channel lead into a loop and solder to top of cross. Run chain through loop.

PEAR ORNAMENT: 1 large, amber, pear-shaped nugget; 3″ square green glass.
1. With felt-tipped pen, outline the shape of 2 leaves on smooth side of green glass. Cut out leaves with glass cutter, following outline.
2. Wrap a single lead channel tightly around amber nugget and leaves individually. Cut lead with razor blade to form close joints.
3. Solder joints of nugget and leaves individually, then solder leaves to top of amber nugget. Turn ornament over and repeat solder joinings on other side.
4. Make a small hanging loop of copper wire and solder to edge of one leaf.

CHERRIES ORNAMENT: 3 large red nuggets; 3″ square green glass.
1. With felt-tipped pen, outline the shape of 2 leaves on smooth side of green glass. Cut out leaves with glass cutter, following outline.
2. Wrap single lead channel tightly around leaves and nuggets individually. Cut lead with razor blade to form close joints.
3. Solder joints of nuggets and leaves individually. Solder nuggets together (2 side by side, the third on the bottom between the other 2); solder leaves together and then solder them to the top of the cherries. Turn ornament over and repeat solder joinings on other side.
4. Make a small hanging loop of copper wire and solder to spot where the 2 leaves join.

BIRD ORNAMENT: 3″ square blue glass; 1 small green nugget.
1. With felt-tipped pen, outline shape of bird's body on smooth side of blue glass. Cut out body with glass cutter, following outline.
2. Wrap single lead channel tightly around body, beginning and ending at tail. Cut lead with razor blade to form a close joint. Wrap single lead channel tightly around green nugget, but leave ½″ of channel free at both start and end of the wrapping for the beak.
3. Solder joint at tip of bird's tail. Solder joint at beak and bend beak ends as shown in photo. Solder lower edge of head in place on body. Turn ornament over and repeat solder joinings on other side.
4. Form a ⅝″ strip of lead channel into a loop and solder to top of head for hanging.

SMALL CHRISTMAS TREE: 5″ square pale amber or pale green glass; small fragments of glass in many colors; clear glass glue.

1. With felt-tipped pen, outline the shape of the Christmas tree on smooth side of pale glass; outline shape of tree pot on smooth side of dark green glass. Cut shapes out with glass cutter, following outlines.

2. Wrap single lead channel tightly around both pieces individually. Cut lead with razor blade to form close joints.

3. Solder joints of tree and tree pot individually. Cut ½" strip of single lead channel for the tree trunk, center it between the pot and the tree and solder in place. Turn ornament over and repeat solder joinings on other side.

4. Place small, various colored pieces of glass between several layers of newspaper and pound with a hammer to make lots of different shapes and sizes.

5. Spread clear glue evenly over one side of Christmas tree and glue the shards of colored glass all over the tree, getting as much color and as many shapes as possible over the area (if there is any glass "sand," sift it between the other pieces to add sparkle and color).

6. Make a small hanging loop of copper wire and solder to back edge of top of tree.

## CHOCOLATE COOKIE ORNAMENTS
*Bake at 350° for 10 minutes.*
*Makes about 4 dozen 3-inch cookies.*

  2 squares unsweetened chocolate
3½ cups *sifted* all purpose flour
  2 teaspoons baking powder
  ½ teaspoon baking soda
  1 teaspoon salt
  ¾ cup (1½ sticks) butter or margarine
  1 cup sugar
  2 eggs
  1 teaspoon vanilla
   Royal Frosting

1. Melt chocolate in a small bowl over hot, not boiling, water; cool.

2. Sift flour, baking powder, baking soda and salt onto wax paper.

3. Beat butter, sugar, eggs, vanilla and cooled chocolate in a large bowl with electric mixer until thoroughly blended. Stir in flour mixture, ⅓ at a time, with a spoon, blending well to make a stiff dough. Wrap in plastic wrap; chill overnight.

4. Divide dough into 4 pieces; roll one piece between two sheets of wax paper to ⅛-inch thickness, lifting top sheet often to dust with

flour and turning dough over for even rolling.

5. Peel off top paper; invert dough onto cookie sheet; peel off paper. Cut into ornament shapes* with floured cookie cutters or cut around your own cardboard pattern with a sharp knife, leaving ½ inch between each cookie for spreading. Carefully lift off dough around cut cookies. Save trimmings and re-roll all at one time. Make a hole in each cookie with a drinking straw.

6. Bake in a moderate oven (350°) for 10 minutes or until cookies are firm. Remove cookies to wire rack with a spatula; cool completely. Store in tightly covered container until decorated.

7. Make Royal Frosting. Decorate cookies as shown in photo; let dry before hanging with ribbons.

*Suggested ornament shapes are bells, tree, scalloped rounds, star, scalloped or plain leaf-shape. To make the long ornaments as shown, take a scalloped round cutter, carefully cut out left and right third of cookie. leaving center of cookie attached. Place small heart-shaped cutter with top rounded-end, overlapping in center third of cookie. Cut out each side towards pointed end. Repeat to cut out opposite side. Use tin cutters to cut out centers of ornaments, if you wish.

## VANILLA COOKIE ORNAMENTS
*Bake at 350° for 8 to 10 minutes. Makes about 5 dozen 3-inch cookies.*

  4 cups *sifted* all purpose flour
  2 teaspoons baking powder
  1 teaspoon salt
  1 cup (2 sticks) butter or margarine
  2 cups sifted 10X (confectioners') sugar
  2 eggs
1½ teaspoons vanilla
   Royal Frosting

1. Sift flour, baking powder and salt onto wax paper.

2. Beat butter with sugar until light and fluffy in a large bowl with electric mixer. Beat in eggs and vanilla. Stir in flour mixture, ⅓ at a time, with a spoon, blending well to make a stiff dough. Wrap dough in plastic wrap; chill overnight.

3. Divide dough into 4 pieces; roll one piece between two sheets of wax paper to ⅛-inch thickness, lifting top sheet often to dust with flour and turning dough over for even rolling.

4. Peel off top paper; invert dough onto cookie sheet; peel off paper. Cut into ornament shapes* with floured cookie cutters or cut around your own cardboard pattern with a sharp knife, leaving ½ inch between each cookie for spreading. Carefully lift off dough around cut cookies. Save trimmings and re-roll all at one time. Make a hole in each cookie with a drinking straw.

5. Bake in moderate oven (350°) for 8 to 10 minutes or until firm and light brown on edges. Remove from cookie sheets to wire racks with wide spatula; cool completely. Store in airtight container until decorated.

6. Make Royal Frosting. Decorate the cookies as shown in photo; let them dry completely before hanging with ribbons.

**ROYAL FROSTING**
*Makes about 2½ cups.*
3 egg whites
1 pound ** *sifted* 10X (confectioners') sugar
1 teaspoon lemon juice

1. Beat egg whites in a medium-size bowl with electric mixer at high speed until soft peaks form.

2. Beat in sugar and lemon juice gradually, and continue to beat until frosting is very stiff. A knife blade should leave a clean sharp line when drawn through. Keep bowl covered with damp paper toweling while working to keep it from hardening. Store any leftover frosting in a screw-top jar.

**For cookies: It may be necessary to use more sugar to make frosting stiff enough to decorate cookies.

*Note:* For iced cookies, thin some of frosting further with water; spread on cookies; sprinkle with colored sugar while wet or allow to dry before decorating. Makes 1 cup.

**CALICO CHRISTMAS-TREE SKIRT**
(about 46″ diameter).
GENERAL INFORMATION: This tree skirt has a patchwork top and plain back with matching ruffles and ties. Synthetic batting is inserted after the top and back have been

seamed and turned. Then the three layers are tufted with sewing thread and red yarn.

MATERIALS: 44″-wide red fabric for back, ruffles, tie and patches, 2¾ yds.; 44″-wide solid gold, red print and green print fabric, ⅓ yd. each; 42″ square piece of synthetic batting; small skein of red yarn; yardstick; tailor's chalk.

DIRECTIONS (½″ seams allowed, unless otherwise indicated):

1. Measure and mark 44″ from one end of red fabric. Cut along mark to make 44″ square for tree skirt Back.
2. From the remaining red fabric mark the following with yardstick and tailor's chalk and cut out: Four ruffle strips each 54″ × 7″; one strip for ties 54″ × 4″ and eighteen 6″ squares. From each of the other three fabrics cut fourteen 6″ squares (to make a total of 60 patches).
3. On a large surface lay out a row of six patches, alternating colors: Below it lay out six rows of eight patches and finish with a row of six patches so you have an 8-row square with the corner patches missing.
4. All patches are joined with ¼″ seams. Seam the patches in each row, to make eight rows. Seam second row to first, matching centers and seams. Continue joining rows to make the complete piece.
5. Fold the patchwork piece in quarters, edges matching, right sides together, and pin edges and folds. At the outside edges make a short pencil mark at each fold to mark the quarters. With a yardstick mark a quarter circle 21″ from the center. Also mark a 3″ quarter circle. Cut out on the inside and outside quarter circle marks through all layers. Cut *one fold only* from outside to inside circles to form a slit. *Do not unfold.*
6. Fold the 44″ red square in quarters. Place the folded skirt top over it, edges matching, and cut the red square the same way to make skirt back. Remove pins.
7. Fold the batting square in quarters and cut in the same way, but make outside circle ½″ smaller and inside circle ½″ larger. Now unfold skirt.

*To make ruffle:*

8. Join the four ruffle pieces at their short ends to make a continuous strip. Fold in half lengthwise, right sides together; seam at each end to make a loop. Turn right side out, fold loop in half lengthwise and press. With largest machine stitch, sew gathering rows ½″ and ⅜″ from raw edges of ruffle, stopping at each seam to cut the thread and begin again.
9. With folded edge inward and raw edges even, pin each end of ruffle to outside curve of skirt top starting ½″ from the slit. Match the ruffle seams to the quarter marks on the skirt and continue pinning, drawing up the gathering rows until the ruffle fits.
10. Fold tie piece in half lengthwise, right sides together and seam at all raw edges. Fold piece in half crosswise and cut on the fold to make two ties. Turn right side out and press.
11. Pin one tie to each edge of slit, ½″ from the inside circle edge, right sides together and raw edges matching. Fold up tie ends and pin to skirt top to keep them from catching in the seams.
12. Pin skirt top to back, right sides together and edges even. Stitch just inside the ruffle stitching and ½″ from other edges, leaving about 15″ open at one edge of slit. Turn right side out. Unpin the ties.
13. Slide batting inside the skirt, working it up to the edges and into the corners. Smooth out and pin through all layers at each patch corner. Turn in opened slit edges and slipstitch closed.
14. Knot one end of strong red sewing thread in needle. From the right side take a stitch through the quilt at each pinmark, bringing needle back up to right side. Take another stitch over one or more 4″ pieces of yarn. Take one more stitch over the yarn and fasten on wrong side. Tie the yarn-ends in a square knot over the sewing thread. Remove pins.

*Color photo on page 71*

## CROSS STITCH TREE SKIRT

MATERIALS: 1⅜ yds. 52″-wide red burlap; 1⅜ yds. 52″-wide backing fabric; 5¼ yds. white covered cording; 4 snap fasteners; knitting worsted in the following colors and amounts: 165 yds. white, 38 yds. emerald, 10 yds. dark green, 4 yds. yellow; sewing thread; tapestry needle; scissors; tailor's chalk.

DIRECTIONS: Cut a 3″ strip from one selvage; cut in half widthwise. Cut a slit from center of burlap to center of one side edge. Stitch half of 3″ strip to one side of slit. Stay-stitch all edges of burlap to prevent raveling. Following directions on page 140, enlarge and trace the design onto burlap, using tailor's chalk. To embroider, use CROSS STITCH (see BASIC EMBROIDERY STITCHES). The crosses are worked over three threads of burlap. Embroider around the work, being careful not to miscount threads. Work all crosses in the same direction, with all underneath stitches going in one direction and all top stitches going in the opposite direction. To begin and end strands, catch yarn under stitches on back of work. Work the trees in green, leaves of pointsetta dark and light green, centers yellow and border, flowers and reindeer white. When embroidery is completed, place the skirt face down and iron, using a damp pressing cloth. Round the corners. On outside, baste or stitch cording along seam line on outer edge, allowing ½″ seam allowance. Prepare backing fabric the same way you prepared the burlap. With right sides together, pin backing to burlap. Sew together, allowing ½″ seam allowance. Leave underneath side of slit open. To form opening for trunk, cut a 3½″ square in center of burlap. Clip corners; turn. Turn edges in between layers. Topstitch burlap and backing together along the slit and around trunk opening. Sew on snap fasteners. Press.

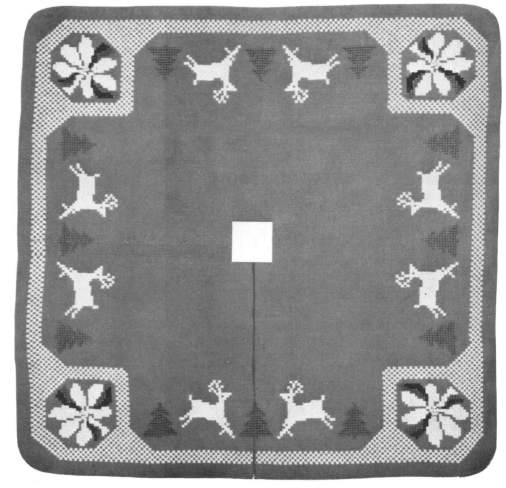

*Color photo on page 71*

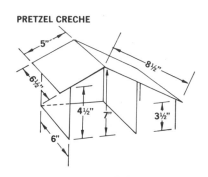

PRETZEL CRECHE

## PRETZEL CRÈCHE

MATERIALS: 22″ × 30″ poster board; Snowy White Frosting (recipe follows); 2 packages (9 ounces each) pretzel rods; 2 packages (6 ounces each) pretzel sticks; 1 package (6 ounces) small pretzel rings; 1 package (6 ounces) small pretzel logs; masking tape; ruler; pencil; compass; X-acto ® knife, razor blade or sharp paring knife; spatula; paper towels; crèche figures (approx. 3″ tall).

DIRECTIONS: Make a 16″ circle on poster board with compass. Mark a 6½″ × 13½″ rectangle for roof, two 4½″ × 6″ rectangles for sides and a 7″ × 7″ piece for back on poster board. Cut out with X-acto ® knife or razor blade. Shape roof by folding 6½″ × 13½″ piece 5″ in from 6½″ edge. Join the two side walls at a 6″ edge to roof with masking tape 3½″ from roof fold, leaving a ½″ overhang at front and rear. Bend roof until two side walls are 6″ apart. Trim the 7″ × 7″ piece to conform to the pitch of the roof. Attach to side walls and roof with masking tape. Prepare SNOWY WHITE FROSTING and cover with a damp paper towel. Spread a thin layer of frosting on back wall with spatula; measure 2 pretzel rods for center of wall to roof and two for side wall joinings; trim rods with X-acto ® knife or sharp paring knife; press into frosting. Select enough pretzel sticks to cover one half of back wall; trim any, if necessary, with X-acto ® knife; press horizontally into frosting. Continue frosting and put pretzels in place until all interior and exterior walls are covered. Place on back edge of posterboard round. Cut 3 pretzel rods long enough to support the two corners and middle of roof overhang; cut 1 pretzel rod long enough to sup-

port the top of roof at crèche opening (*Note*: This is just used while crèche is made and dries. It will then be removed.) Cut 2 pretzel rods to fit side wall edges. Cut 1 pretzel rod to fit along top of roof. Frost top and bottom of the 3 pretzel rods and press into cardboard base and roof at both corners and in center of roof side with overhang. Insert rod for roof support at crèche opening, but do not frost. Frost side wall edges and press pretzel rods in place. Starting at left roof edge, spread a 2″ layer of frosting from front to back. Lay a row of pretzel sticks, overhanging roof by ½″. Allow to dry 15 minutes. Make a 2″-wide strip of paper towels as thick as pretzel sticks; cover next 2″ of roof with frosting; press paper towel strip into place; frost to coat completely. Lay a row of pretzel sticks to cover paper towel strips completely. Allow to dry 15 minutes. Continue laying paper towel strips and pretzel sticks until roof is completely covered, trimming pretzel sticks to fit on row near top of roof. Make a small stack of pretzel logs at side of crèche, using frosting to keep in place. Spread a layer of frosting from crèche to front of poster-board round in a swirling pattern; press pretzel sticks in place to make a path. Crush remaining pretzels, except pretzel rounds. Spread remaining frosting on poster-board. Press pretzel rounds into frosting to make a fence at either side of crèche. Press crushed pretzels into frosting to cover completely. Allow to dry overnight.

SNOWY WHITE FROSTING: Makes enough to frost crèche. Beat 6 egg whites until foamy white and double in volume in large bowl of electric mixer at high speed. Beat in 2 pounds 10X (confectioners' powdered) sugar gradually until mixture forms stiff peaks. Keep frosting covered with a damp paper towel while building and decorating crèche.

(see page 4)

(see page 8)

(see page 7)

66

(see page 25)

(see page 16)

(see page 12)

(see page 22

(see page 31)

ee page 29)

(see page 29)

(see page 33)

68

(see page 36)

(see page 38)

(see page ‹

(see page 44)

69

(see page 49)

(see page 46)

70

(see page 55)

(see page 51)

(see page 40)

(see page 61)

(see page 64)

72

(see page 82)

(see page 81

(see page 84)

(see page 90

73

(see page 88)

(see page 87)

(see page 91)

74

(see page 93)

(see
page 100)

(see page

(see page 101)

ee page 103)

(see page 105)

76

(see page 103)

(see page 101)

(see page 101)

(see page 106)

(see page 1

(see page 116)

78

(see page 130)

(see page 109)

(see page 11

(see page 127)

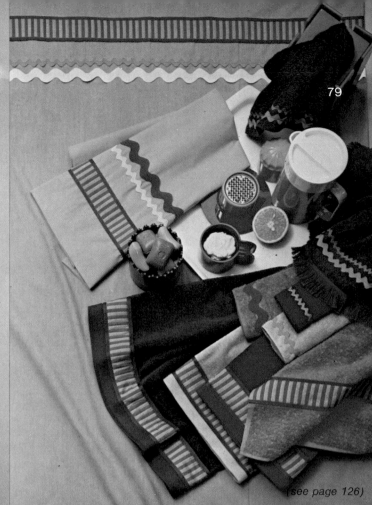

(see page 126)

see page 125)

(see page 121)

80

*(see page 136)*

*(see page 134)*

# Gifts for the Family

## For the Lady of the House

### SEWING CADDY

Make this sewing caddy from a frosting or baking powder can. With white glue, secure pincushion to lid; cover can with tape measure strips, slightly overlapping tape at the ends.

### MOTHER—DAUGHTER APRONS

Directions are given for Woman's size. Changes for Child's size are in parentheses. MATERIALS: (for both aprons): 1 yd. 45"-wide muslin-type heavy cotton; remnants of red print fabrics; 4 yds. red double-fold bias tape; red thread; natural thread; scissors; measuring tape; pencil; paper for pattern. CUTTING MEASUREMENTS—*Woman's Size*: Body and pockets, 24" wide × 24" high; waistband, 3½"×21"; ties, two 3"×20". *Child's Size:* Body and pockets, 18" wide × 16" high; waistband, 3½"×15"; ties, two 3"×16". DIRECTIONS: Mark the pockets by basting a line 7(5)" from the bottom, across the width. (This is the fold line.) Divide with two basting lines into three pockets 8(6)" wide. Baste tape on the two vertical basting lines, even with the raw edge and 1" over the fold line. Stitch across tape on fold line to secure. Bind top edge of pockets, enclosing raw ends of vertical tapes. Following directions on page

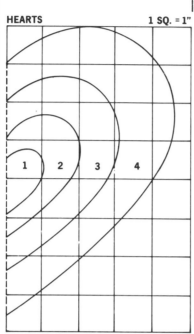

HEARTS                    1 SQ. = 1"

1  2  3  4

*Color photo on page 72*

*Color photo on page 72*

140, enlarge and cut out Size 3 (Size 2) heart. Cut out three hearts for each apron. Fold up pockets and pin hearts in place, centered on each pocket. Appliqué hearts in place, making sure to appliqué through only one layer of fabric. Pin folded-up pockets in place. Stitch along both edges of tapes separating pockets, through tapes and the two layers of fabric. Bind side edges of apron. Form two pleats ½" deep and 1" apart, 4½(3½)" from side edges. Fold ties in half lengthwise, wrong side out. Stitch ½" seam on long edges and one short end. Trim edges, turn. Stitch other short end closed. Place waistband on wrong side of apron, one long edge flush with apron top edge. Stitch a ½" seam. Insert ties and baste in place, folding side edges of waistband under ½". Turn other long edge of waistband under ½" and baste to apron front. On right side of waistband, stitch one row close to all edges.

## PAN HANDLER
MATERIALS: Scraps of quilted fabric; 2" or 3" scrap of bias tape for loop; straight pins; scissors.
DIRECTIONS: Cut 2 scraps of quilted fabric 9"×4". Round off corners on one end. On other end, turn under ½" on each, stitch in place. Fold bias tape in half to form a loop,

wrong sides facing; stitch. Pin in place. With right sides facing, stitch quilted pieces together with ¼" seam, leaving short, straight end open. Clip; turn right side out. Topstitch with ¼" seam.

## SEWING AIDS
From sawdust and felt scraps, make three pincushions: A green pear, 4" long; a pink 1" ball with 3" cerise petals; one egg, 2" high. Decorate each as shown in photo. Sew *pear* to end of yard-long ribbon with shears at other end. Stitch *flower* to velvet-covered elastic wristband. Glue egg-shaped *rooster* in an egg cup.

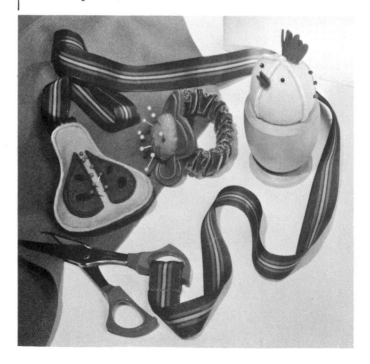

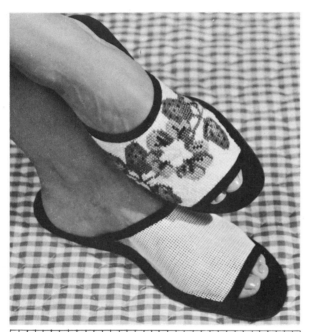

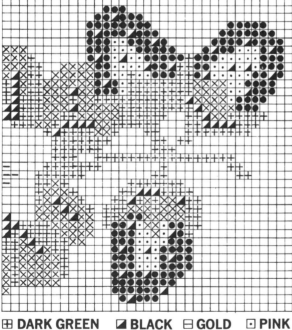

⊞ **DARK GREEN**   ◪ **BLACK**   ⊟ **GOLD**   ⊡ **PINK**
⊠ **LIGHT GREEN**   ☐ **WHITE**   ⊙ **RED**

## NEEDLEPOINT SLIPPERS

MATERIALS: Soft fabric slippers; scraps of No. 10 mono canvas; Dark green, black, gold, pink, light green, white and red needlepoint yarn; tapestry needle.

DIRECTIONS: With Continental Stitch (*see* BASIC NEEDLEPOINT STITCHES), work motif on No. 10 mono canvas, using color key given with chart, then sew the blocked, trimmed-to-fit canvas onto soft fabric slippers.

## SEED PENDANTS

*Note:* You'll have to start a bit early on this one—it may take some time to collect the cantaloupe seeds if you plan on more than one pendant. Generally, the seeds from two to three melons should provide enough to cover one disc.

### DISC PENDANTS

MATERIALS: For each disc: 1½"-diameter round of cardboard or thin wood; cantaloupe seeds, cleaned and dried; dried green split peas and whole barley (optional); white glue and clear plastic spray; scissors; thin wire. For seed chain: additional cantaloupe seeds, needle and clear nylon fishing line.

DIRECTIONS: Discs: Starting at outer edge of cardboard or wood circle, apply a thin layer of glue. While the glue is still moist, place cantaloupe seeds around edge with the seeds pointed toward the center. (Tweezers are helpful in applying seeds.) Apply more glue; add another row of seeds. Repeat procedure, one row at a time, until entire surface is covered with seeds. If you wish, glue down a small row of split peas in the center. Let glue dry thoroughly. Glue a row of barley around outside of peas (optional). Spray with clear plastic for shiny protective finish. Cut a small wire loop; glue to back of pendant. *To String Pendants:* For seeded cord, simply thread needle with fishing line and poke it through centers of cantaloupe seeds to string them until desired length is reached. Slip one end of fishing line through loop on pendant; knot with other end. Clip off excess fishing line and push seeds down to cover knot. Coat seed chain with clear plastic spray.

### CIRCULAR PENDANT

MATERIALS: Cantaloupe seeds, cleaned and dried (about ½ cup); copper wire; wire clippers; clear plastic spray.

DIRECTIONS: Bend a piece of wire into a 1½"-diameter circle, so there is a 1" excess remaining at beginning and end of circle. Prick holes through centers of seeds; slip seeds onto wire circle to cover; twist both wire overlaps together twice to close circle, then form them into a single loop. Chain is 1½" sections of wire, strung with seeds and connected to one another with loops at either end. Attach chain to loop on disc. Coat with clear plastic spray.

*Color photo on page 72*

## SPLIT PEA BOX

MATERIALS: Wooden box with lid (available in hobby and crafts stores); dried green and yellow split peas; white glue and clear plastic spray.

DIRECTIONS: Draw a line design on box top and sides. (Ours was a series of diagonal lines, evenly spaced.) Spread a thin layer of white glue over the design, a small area at a time. While glue is still moist, place peas, split side down, on glue over pencil lines, alternating green and yellow in desired pattern. When design is complete, let glue dry thoroughly, several hours or overnight. Spray box with clear plastic; let dry.

## CLAY JEWELRY

RECIPE FOR CLAY: Mix 1 cup cornstarch and 2 cups baking soda in top of double boiler. Add 1¼ cups water and cook until consistency of mashed potatoes. Spoon onto a plate and cover with a wet towel. When cool, knead like dough and divide into 4 balls. Color 3 of the balls by kneading in a teaspoon or more of Rit powdered dye (turquoise, chestnut brown, and a mixture of tangerine and golden yellow). Use the white ball to lighten the other colors. You can marbleize the clay as desired by mixing one or more of the colored clays (or white) together.

CLAY BEADS:

1. *Ball:* Roll the clay into a small ball in the palm of your hand. Allow to dry a little, then make a hole through the center with a large needle. Allow to harden.

2. *Disc:* Roll a small or medium (depending on what jewelry you are making calls for) ball in the palm of your hand and flatten with your finger. Make a hole through the center with a needle. Allow to harden.

3. *Sausage:* Roll the clay into sausages about ⅝" long with your fingers. Make a hole through the length with needle. Allow to harden.

4. *Oval:* Roll a small amount into a sausage and flatten. Make holes with the needle (as many as the piece of jewelry calls for) through the thickness. Allow to harden.

5. *Tube:* Pack desired length of clay into a plastic drinking straw by picking it up with the straw. Squeeze out like toothpaste by pressing straw in your fingers. Cut ends of clay clean with a small knife. Allow to harden a little, then make a hole through the length. Allow to harden.

METAL BEADS

MATERIALS: Sheet of 36 gauge aluminum 1×3 feet; pizza cutter or dressmaker's tracing wheel; scissors.

DIRECTIONS: Make a texture in the aluminum sheet by rolling a pizza cutter or dressmaker's tracing wheel lightly over it.

1. *Leaf:* With a pencil, outline the shape of a leaf about 2×½" with a 2" strip on the top. Scratch in leaf lines with an awl or the blunt end of a sewing needle. Cut out and roll strip into a tube with small pliers.

2. *Disc:* With a pencil, outline a 1¼" circle with a 1¾"×¼" strip. Cut out and roll strip into a tube with small pliers. Make a small hole in middle of circle.

3. *Tube:* Cut strips of aluminum 1¼" long × ½" or ¼" wide (depending on what jewelry you are making calls for). Roll strips into tubes with small pliers.

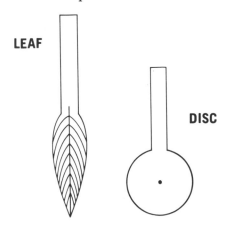

**LEAF**

**DISC**

## LEAF NECKLACE

MATERIALS: 3 lengths of fishing line, each 2½′ long. *Aluminum beads:* seven leaf beads; fourteen ¼″ tube beads; four ½″ tube beads; twenty-two aluminum ⅜″ washers. *Clay beads:* forty-four small ball beads; fourteen 1″ tube beads; six ¾″ tube beads; six ⅝″ tube beads; two 1″ flat oval beads (with 3 holes); twenty-four ⅜″ disc beads; liquid plastic.

DIRECTIONS:

1. String a leaf on the center of one length of fishing line. String a ball bead on either side, followed by a 1″ clay tube bead and another ball bead. Repeat pattern on both sides until you have used the 7 leaves (see photo).

2. Repeat design for second strand using ¼″ aluminum beads in place of leaves, and ¾″ clay tubes in place of the 1″ tubes. Repeat for 3rd (top) strand, again with ¼″ aluminum beads but this time using ⅝″ clay tubes.

3. String each end of the 3 strands through the 3 holes of the 2 flat oval beads (one on each side). String one ball on each end of the middle strand and one ½″ aluminum bead on each end of top and bottom strands.

4. String flat disc beads (12 on each side) alternately with washers (11 on each side) over all 3 strands. Tie ends in a double square knot and cut 2 strands on each end short. String four 1″ tube beads on each end of remaining strand.

5. Tie ends together and coat all beads with liquid plastic.

## SINGLE STRAND NECKLACE

MATERIALS: 3′ length of fishing line. *Clay beads:* twenty-one ½″ sausage beads; four ¾″ tube beads; eleven 1¼″ tube beads; four ½″ disc beads; one ⅝″ disc bead; one flat oval bead (about 1¼″) with 2 holes. *Aluminum beads:* Fourteen ¼″ tube beads; six ½″ tube beads; one 1¼″ disc; 1 aluminum wire, cut in half.

DIRECTIONS:

1. String a sausage bead on the center of the fishing line. String one ½″ aluminum tube bead on either side of sausage bead.

2. String a matching pattern of beads on either side of brass beads, using photo as a guide. End with a 1¼″ clay tube bead.

3. Take the ⅝″ clay disc bead and half the wire. String the wire through the hole in the bead; bring the wire around one side of the

bead and through hole again and around other side of the bead (in a figure 8 pattern). Bring wire up to meet other end and twist ends together once.

4. Cut one end of the wire short. String remaining end through hole in aluminum disc and make a small loop against the back of the disc to hold it in place. Trim end of wire.

5. Thread the remaining 6″ of wire through strip on disc. String one clay ball on each side of strip.

6. Thread wire through the 2 holes in the flat oval bead and then through the two center ½″ aluminum beads on necklace (*see photo*). Trim wire to about ¼″ and curl ends. Coat beads with 2 coats of liquid plastic.

## CLOTHESLINE CRAFTS

GENERAL DIRECTIONS: *Basic Wrap Technique:* To begin, thread needle with doubled length of yarn (or thread, or cord); wrap yarn tightly around clothesline (as shown). *Changing colors:* To begin a new length of yarn or to change yarn color, run needle back under last few wraps, about 1″; cut yarn off closely. Begin wrapping with next piece ¼″ to ½″ over end of wrapped section. (This method eliminates loose ends.) *Joining:* To stitch or fasten rounds or coils of clothesline to each other, as you wrap bare piece of clothesline, run needle under yarn of wrapped piece of clothesline every 3 or 4 wraps. *To finish an item:* When you have wrapped up to

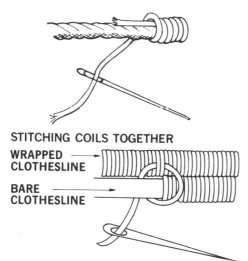

STITCHING COILS TOGETHER

WRAPPED →
CLOTHESLINE

BARE →
CLOTHESLINE

1" from point where you want to finish, cut off clothesline; wrap and stitch over end of clothesline until securely attached and no bare clothesline is visible.

## WOMAN'S BELT

Directions are for 29" belt. Adjust clothesline lengths for desired size, remembering that there are 6 coils of clothesline to adjust for extra length.

MATERIALS: Tapestry needle; 20 feet of ¼"-diameter clothesline or rope; double-ply wool yarn in the following colors and amounts: 14 yards cream, 15 yards red, 15 yards tan, 15 yards navy, 18 yards blue; 18 yards lavender double-ply cotton yarn; 2 hooks (⅜") and eyes.

*Note:* For varied effects, use yarns with different textures.

DIRECTIONS: Following General Directions for basic wrapping and color change techniques, and using cream yarn, wrap length of

clothesline to desired length of belt (ours was 29"). Change to lavender; wrap 3"; bend clothesline (as shown by (A) in diagram); stitch 2 pieces of clothesline together by wrapping and stitching around coils 6 times. Wrap 5" more; bend to form second loop (B); secure by stitching 2 pieces to each other; continue wrapping, making stitches where indicated on diagram. Continue wrapping and stitching lavender to cream length of clothesline; change to red yarn when second length of clothesline is as long as first. Bend clothesline around end of first length; wrap and stitch third length, allowing 3 gaps where coils are not stitched together, each 3" long and 1½" apart, at back of belt *(see diagram)*. At end of belt, bend clothesline around loops, stitching every 4 or 5 wraps; change to tan at end of biggest loop; complete tan length. Bend clothesline around end of belt; change to navy and wrap and stitch to red length; change to blue when you reach the first of the loops at other end of belt. Follow shape of loops, leaving unstitched openings (as shown in diagram); complete

## WOMAN'S BELT

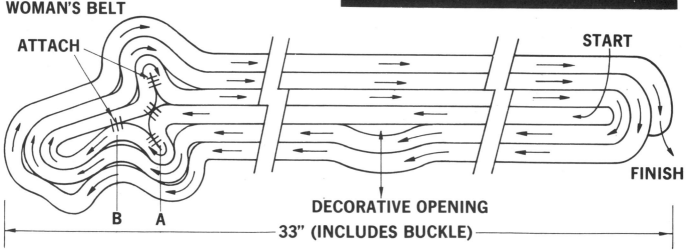

ATTACH

START

B    A

DECORATIVE OPENING

FINISH

33" (INCLUDES BUCKLE)

blue length; cut clothesline off at end of blue length. Try on belt; sew on hooks and eyes where desired.

NECKPIECE

MATERIALS: Tapestry needle; 6 ft. of ³/₁₆″-diameter Venetian-blind cord or rope; 27 ft. cream double-ply twisted cord; 12 ft. blue 8 cord-cable twist cotton; 2 ft. grey double-ply wool yarn; 6 ft. dark green satin cord; 3 ft. light blue 8 cord-cable twist cotton; 10 ft. rose heavy-weight cotton thread; 5 ft. lavender heavy-weight cotton thread; 3 ft. turquoise double-ply wool yarn; 2 small clay beads, 3 small wooden beads and 1 large wooden bead (optional).

DIRECTIONS: Neckpiece is worked in two main sections: the basic choker section, and the ornament. For choker, cut a 36″ length of cord or rope. Following BASIC WRAP TECHNIQUE, begin wrapping with cream cord; wrap 4″; change to blue cotton; wrap ½″; change to grey; wrap ½″; change back to cream for 1½″; change to green satin and wrap for 1″; change to turquoise for 1″; leave ½″ unwrapped, pulling last of turquoise thread along so it will not hang loose; wrap 1″ of rose and lavender combined; bending cord in the middle of this color section, as shown in diagram. After rose/lavender, change to light

blue, and wrap over *both* sides of doubled cord *(see diagram)* for ½″; change to turquoise for ¼″, then continue with turquoise over both (doubled) sides for ¼″, then back to the one side for another ¼″, making sure that this side of neckpiece matches the first wrapped half; change to green satin for 1″; change to cream and complete the rest of the neckpiece section in reverse order to match the first side. When both sides measure evenly, continue wrapping in cream to make a button loop as shown; wrap with cream for 4″ more, stitching the two (doubled) cords together every ¾″, as shown in diagram. Change to light blue for ¼″, then to grey for ¼″, then back to cream for 1″, stitching doubled cord together every 2 or 3 wraps (as outlined in basic wrap technique for Joining). Change to green satin for 1½″, curving cord as necessary; change to light blue for ¼″; wrap light blue around both cords for ¼″ as shown; repeat; continue light blue for ¼″ more; change to rose/lavender around both cords for ¼″; wrap 1″ of turquoise yarn (this will be center point on neckpiece). Finish second half of neckpiece in reverse order to match; when you reach starting point, cut off cord and tie off end. Cut an 18″ piece of cord for ornament. Beginning 4″ down from start of neckpiece, wrap ornament cord in the following color pattern, curving it as shown in diagram, and stitching it to neckpiece as you work: 1½″ cream, ½″ lavender, ½″ rose, 1″ cream, 2″ light blue, ½″ rose, 2″ green satin, ¼″ rose, 1″ turquoise wool, ½″ cream; repeat this order in reverse for second half. When both sides are completed, secure end of ornament to neckpiece. To finish, sew on beads where indicated.

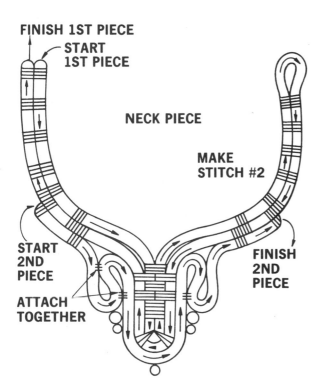

*Color photo on page 73*

## MULTICOLOR VICTORIAN POUCH

Pouch measures 9″, plus tassel.

MATERIALS: DMC Cotton #5: 4 balls Ecru (A), 2 balls each of #3347 (B) and #815 (C); 1 ball each of #972 (D) and #352 (E); crochet hook, size E, *or any size hook which will obtain the stitch gauge below.*

GAUGE: 8 sts =1″.

*Pouch:* Starting at lower end with A ch 4. Join with sl st to form a ring. *Rnd 1:* 9 sc in ring. Join with sl st to first sc. *Rnd 2:* Ch 1, 2 sc in same sc used for joining, 2 sc in each sc around. Join with sl st to first sc—18 sc. *Rnd 3:* Ch 1, sc in same sc as joining, *2 sc in next sc, sc in next sc; rpt from * around, end with 2 sc in last sc. Join—9 sc inc. *Rnd 4:* Ch 1, sc in same sc as joining, sc in next sc, *2 sc in next sc, sc in each of next 2 sc; rpt from * around, end 2 sc in last sc. Join—36 sc. *Rnd 5:* Ch 1, sc in same sc as joining, sc in next 2 sc, *2 sc in next sc, sc in next 3 sc; rpt from * around, end 2 sc in last sc. Join. *Rnds 6 and 7:* Ch 1, sc in same sc as joining and in each sc around. Join—45 sc. *Rnd 8:* Ch 3 to count as 1 dc, 2 dc in same sc as joining, 3 dc in each sc around. Join to top of ch-3—135 dc. *Rnds 9 through 14:* Ch 3, sk joining, dc in each dc around. Join to top of ch-3. *Rnd 15:* Ch 3, sk joining, *dc in each of next 5 dc, holding back on hook last loop of each dc, dc in each of next 2 dc, thread over hook and draw through all 3 loops on hook—*dec made;* rpt from * 17 more times; dc in each rem dc. Join—117 dc. *Rnd 16:* Rpt Rnd 6. *Rnd 17:* Ch 3, place a strand of B along top edge of last rnd, with A, working over B, dc in next 3 dc, *holding back on hook last loop, dc in next dc, drop A, draw a B loop through loops on hook—*color change made;* holding back on hook last loop, with B dc in next dc, drop B, pick up A and draw a loop through loops on hook (always make color change in this manner), with A, working over B, dc in next 7 dc; rpt from * around, end with A dc in last 4 dc. Join. Starting with Rnd marked 18, follow Diagram 1, repeating from right to left around each rnd. Always carry color not in use inside sts; change color in last dc of each color group. When a color is no longer in use, break off. At end of Rnd 24, break off both strands and fasten. Attach C to same st used for joining. *Rnds 25 and 26:* With C, sc in same st as joining and in each st around. Join to first sc. Break off and fasten

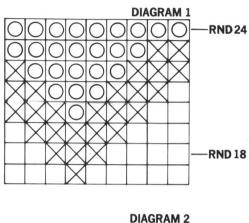

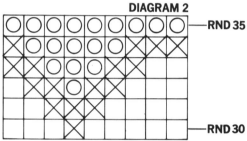

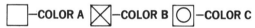

*Color photo on page 73*

at end of last rnd. Attach D. *Rnds 27 and 28:* With D, rpt last 2 rnds. Break off and fasten. Attach A. *Rnd 29:* Rpt Rnd 9. *Rnds 30 through 35:* Follow Diagram 2. At end of last rnd break off B and C. *Rnds 36 and 37:* With A, rpt Rnd 9, inc 1 dc on last rnd—118 dc. *Rnd 38:* Ch 6, *sk next dc, tr in next dc, ch 2; rpt from * around, end with sk last dc. Join to 4th ch of ch-6. *Rnd 39:* Ch 2, *2 hdc in next sp, ch 3, sl st in top of last st for picot; rpt from * around. Join to top of ch-2. Break off and fasten.

*Drawstring*: With 2 strands of A held tog, make a chain 28″ long. Sc in 2nd ch from hook and in each ch across. Ch 1, turn. Sc in each sc across. Break off and fasten. Weave cord through sps of Rnd 38.

*Tassel*: Wind A 100 times around a 4″ piece of cardboard, tie at one end, cut at opposite end. Wind and tie a separate strand around tassel, ½″ below tied end. Trim evenly. Tack to starting ring at bottom of pouch.

## CROCHETED BODICE WITH PEPLUM

Directions are given for size Small (6-8). Changes for size Medium (10-12) are in parentheses.

MATERIALS: Bucilla Paradise (1 oz. sks): 10 (12) skeins; crochet hook, Size F, *or any size hook which will obtain the stitch gauge below.*

GAUGE: 9 dc = 2″; 5 rows = 2″.

| MEASUREMENTS: | | |
|---|---|---|
| SIZES: | SMALL | MEDIUM |
| | (6–8) | (10–12) |
| BODY BUST SIZE: | 29″–31½″ | 31½″–33″ |

*Front*: Starting at waist (peplum will be added later), ch 56 (68) to measure 13″ (15″). *Next Row*: Dc in 6th ch from hook, * ch 1, sk next ch, dc in next ch. Rpt from * across—26 (32) sps. Ch 4, turn and work in pat as follows: *Row 1* (right side): Sk first dc and ch-1, * holding back on hook the last loop of each dc, make 3 dc in next dc, yarn over hook and draw through all 4 loops on hook—*cluster made*; (ch 1, dc in next dc) twice; ch 1. Rpt from * across ending with ch 1, cluster in last dc, ch 1, sk next ch of turning chain, dc in next ch—9 (11) clusters. Ch 4, turn. *Row 2*: Sk first dc, * dc in top of next cluster (ch 1, dc in next dc) twice; ch 1. Rpt from * across ending with ch 1, dc in last cluster, ch 1, sk next ch of turning chain, dc in next ch—26 (32) sps. Ch 4, turn. Rpt Rows 1 and 2 alternately 5 (6) times; then rpt Row 1 once more. Ch 3, turn. *Inc Row*: 2 dc in each of next 3 (8) sps, 3 dc in each of next 7 (5) sps, * dc in top of next cluster (ch 1, dc in next dc) twice; ch 1. Rpt from * once; dc in next cluster, 3 dc in each of next 7 (5) sps, 2 dc in each of next 3 (8) sps, dc in top of ch-3—58 (66) dc plus 6 sps in center. Ch 3, turn. *Next Row*: Sk first dc, dc in each dc across to center sps; over center sps make 2 sps, ch 1, cluster in center dc, make 3 sps, dc in each dc across, dc in top of ch-3—same number sts as on last row. Ch 3, turn. *Following Row*: Sk first dc, dc in each dc across to center sps; over center sps make 2 sps, ch 1, dc in center cluster, make 3 sps, dc in each dc, dc in top of ch-3. Ch 3, turn. Rpt last 2 rows alternately 3 times. Ch 4, turn. *Next Row*: Sk first 2 dc, dc in 3rd dc. ON MEDIUM SIZE ONLY: (Ch 1, sk next dc, dc in next dc) twice. ON BOTH SIZES: * Ch 1, sk next dc, cluster in next dc, (ch 1, sk next dc, dc in next dc) twice. Rpt from * across dc's and center panel ending with 2 (4) sps after last cluster. Place a marker in both ends of last row to indicate end of side seam. Ch 4, turn.

*Upper Right Front: Row 1*: (Dc in next dc) 1 (3) times; * dc in next cluster, (ch 1, dc in next dc) twice; ch 1, Rpt from * once; dc in next cluster—this is neck edge. Ch 3, turn. *Row 2*: Cluster in first dc, * (ch 1, dc in next dc) twice; ch 1, cluster in next dc. Rpt from * once; ch 1 and complete row in pat. Ch 4, turn. Rpt Rows 1 and 2 alternately 5 (6)

times. At end of last row, fasten off.

*Upper Left Front:* Skip next 5 clusters on last row before Upper Right Front, attach yarn in top of next cluster, ch 4 and work to correspond with other side.

*Back:* Work same as Front to within Inc Row. Ch 3, turn. *Inc Row:* In first sp make 4 (2) dc; 2 dc in 1 (2) sps; * 3 dc in next sp, 2 dc in next sp. Rpt from * 10 (12) more times; 3 (2) dc in next 2 sps, dc in turning chain—69 (77) dc. Ch 3, turn. *Next Row:* Sk first dc, dc in each dc across, dc in top of ch-3—69 (77) dc. Ch 3, turn. Rpt last row 7 times. Ch 4, turn. *Next Row:* Sk first 2 dc, dc in 3rd dc. ON MEDIUM SIZE ONLY: (Ch 1, sk next dc, dc in next dc) twice. ON BOTH SIZES: * Ch 1, sk next dc, cluster in next dc, (ch 1, sk next dc, dc in next dc) twice. Rpt from * across ending with 2 (4) sps after last cluster. Place a marker in both ends of last row. Ch 4, turn. Work even in pat as established, until same number of rows have been made above markers as are on Front above markers. For shoulder, work over 8 (10) sps. Fasten off. Sk next 18 sps, attach yarn and work over rem 8 (10) sps. Fasten off. Sew shoulder seams.

*Sleeves: Row 1:* Attach yarn on wrong side in the top of end st of marked row. Working along armhole edge in ends of rows, ch 4, * dc in top of st at end of next row, ch 1. Rpt from * across to next marker. Ch 4, turn. *Row 2:* Dc in next dc, * ch 1, cluster in next dc, (ch 1, dc in next dc) twice. Rpt from * across. Ch 4, turn. *Row 3:* Work sps over sps and clusters as before. Ch 4, turn. Rpt Rows 2 and 3 alternately 12 times; then rpt Row 2 once more. Ch 3, turn.

*Ruffle: Row 1:* * 2 dc in next sp, dc in next dc (or cluster as the case may be). Rpt from * across. Ch 4, turn. Rpt Rows 2 and 3 of Sleeve twice; then rpt Row 2 once more. Ch 4, turn. *Last Row:* In first dc make tr, ch 1 and dc; ch 1, in each dc and cluster across make dc, ch 1, tr, ch 1, dc and ch 1. Fasten off. Sew sleeve seams and right side seam.

*Peplum:* Work same as Ruffle on Sleeve along lower edge.

*Front Frill:* With right side facing, attach yarn to the top of the 2nd dc to the left of center cluster on front neck edge. Ch 4, in same place where yarn was attached make tr, ch 1 and dc, * ch 1, in top of next dc on row below make *dc, ch 1, tr, ch 1 and dc—shell*

*made.* Rpt from * across to first cluster row of Front above Peplum; then, working parallel to lower edge, make a shell in base of each of the next dc, cluster and dc; then make shells along 2nd row of dc's on other side of center cluster to neck edge; sl st to neck edge. Fasten off.

*Neck Frill:* Work shells in each dc and cluster along entire neck edge. Fasten off. Sew left side seam.

## WOVEN RIBBON VEST AND BAG

*Note:* Materials are given for Misses Size 10. For other sizes, adjust ribbon yardages by measuring pattern piece for vest front.

MATERIALS: McCall's pattern #5723 Misses Vest; 1 yard 36″ wide muslin; ½ yard 36″ wide velvet; 1 yard 45″ wide satin lining fabric, scissors; pins; 1 covered snap; ribbons in the following colors, widths and amounts: 4⅔″ yards 1″ wide shocking pink grosgrain (A); 1¾″ yards ¼″ wide maroon velvet (B1); 2⅔ yards 1″ wide maroon velvet (B2); 1¾″yards 1⅛″ wide maroon floral (C1); 2¼ yards ¾″ wide maroon floral (C2); 5⅓ yards 1″ wide maroon satin (D); 3 yards ¼″ wide shocking pink velvet (E); ¾ yard 1″ wide hot pink grosgrain (F); ⅚ yard ¼″ wide raspberry velvet (G).

*Color photo on page 72*

DIRECTIONS:

VEST: Cut 2 vest fronts of muslin, which will be used as base for weaving the ribbons. Cut

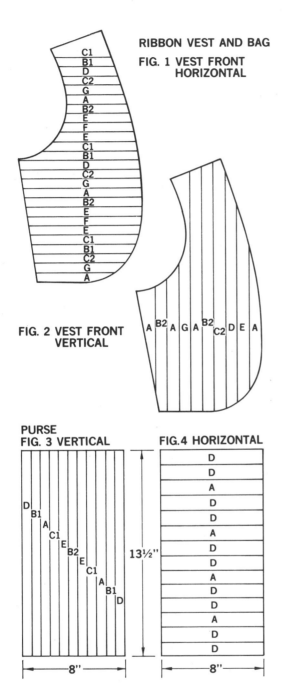

**RIBBON VEST AND BAG**

**FIG. 1 VEST FRONT HORIZONTAL**

C1
B1
D
C2
G
A
B2
E
F
E
C1
B1
D
C2
G
A
B2
E
F
E
C1
B1
D
C2
G
A

**FIG. 2 VEST FRONT VERTICAL**

A B2 A G A B2 C2 D E A

**PURSE**
**FIG. 3 VERTICAL**

D
B1
A
C1
E
B2
E
C1
A
B1
D

**FIG. 4 HORIZONTAL**

D
D
A
D
D
A
D
D
A
D
D
A
D
D
A
D
D

13½"

8"

8"

and pin ribbons in place on vest front piece as show in Fig. 1 (Horizontal). Working in the Vertical as shown in Fig. 2, weave ribbons in over-under lattice pattern. Pin ribbons in place; stitch all around edge of woven ribbon vest front ⅜" from edge. Work other vest front in the same way. Cut vest back piece from velvet fabric. Stitch vest fronts to velvet back at side seams only, leaving shoulder seams to be stitched after lining has been set in. Cut satin lining, using front and back pattern pieces (cut one back on fold and cut 2

pieces of front). Stitch side seams of lining; press open, leaving shoulder seams of lining to be stitched later. Pin, right sides together (Front, Back and lining); stitch, allowing ⅝" for seam, except for shoulder seams. Turn right side out and press carefully. Machine stitch shoulder seams of vest and hand stitch satin lining to finish.

PURSE
(Finished size: 5"×7½".) Cut one muslin piece 8"×13½" as base for weaving ribbons. Pin ribbons in place as shown in Fig. 3 (Vertical). Turn piece and work in Horizontal direction as shown in Fig. 4. Stitch ¼" in from edge to hold in place. Fold woven piece 5" up from one short edge with right sides together; stitch the two sides ¼" from edge. Cut satin piece same size as muslin. Pin right side of woven piece to right side of lining; stitch ¼" around the 3 sides, leaving one short side open; turn; hand stitch lining to purse at opening. Sew on snap for closing.

**SHAWL WITH RIBBON INSERTION**
Shawl measures approximately 25"×60", plus fringe.
MATERIALS: Unger's Loop d Loop (1.85 oz. skeins): 10 skeins Natural; knitting needles, Scoville-Hero No. 20, *or any size needles which will obtain the stitch gauge below;* 1½ yds. each of 6 colors of grosgrain ribbon, ⅞"-wide: Rust, Dark Yellow, Green, Maroon, Pink and Fudge Brown (or any 6 colors); large crochet hook for fringe.
GAUGE: 5 sts = 3"; 6 rows of pat = 3".
DIRECTIONS: Starting at one narrow edge, cast on 41 sts. K 3 rows for border. Work in pat as follows: *Row 1 (right side):* K 1, *yo, k 1; rpt from * across. *Row 2:* K across, dropping all yo of previous row so that each st becomes elongated. *Rows 3 through 6:* K 4 rows. Rpt last 6 rows (Rows 1 through 6) for pat. Work in pat until length is 60" from beg, ending with k 3 rows. Bind off loosely.
*Finishing:* Pin shawl to measurements on a padded surface, cover with a damp cloth and allow to dry; do not press.
*Fringe:* Wind yarn several times around a 5" square of cardboard, cut at one end, making 10" strands. Continue to cut strands as needed. Fold 1 strand in half to form a loop. With right side facing insert crochet hook from back to front in first st at one narrow edge

*Color photo on page 73*

and draw loop through, draw loose ends through loop and pull tightly to form a knot. Tie one strand in same way in each st across narrow edge. Tie fringe along opposite edge in same manner.

*Ribbon Insertion:* Cut each 1½-yd. piece of ribbon in half. Starting with Rust, draw ribbon through first row of elongated sts, drawing ribbon over one st, then under next st across width of shawl. Fold back ends of ribbon to wrong side and fasten neatly and securely in place. Draw ribbon in same manner through each of next 5 elongated st rows in the following sequence: Dark Yellow, Green, Maroon Pink and Fudge Brown. Repeat opposite end.

## GRANNY SQUARE THROW/SHAWL

Directions are given for finished throw measuring 41″×78″ including fringe.

MATERIALS: Bucilla Melody 1 oz. balls No. 1 Crystal White, 20 balls; crochet hook, Size F, *or any size hook which will obtain the stitch gauge below;* tapestry needle No. 18.

GAUGE: Each 3-round motif measures 3¾″×3¾″.

*Motif (make 187):* Starting at center, ch 4. Join with sl st to form ring. *Rnd 1:* Ch 3, in ring make 2 dc, ch 2 and (3 dc, ch 2) 3 times. Join with sl st to top of ch-3. *Rnd 2:* Sl st in next 2 dc, sl st in sp, ch 3, in same sp make 2 dc, ch 2 for corner sp and 3 dc; (ch 1, in next sp make 3 dc, ch 2 for corner sp and 3 dc) 3 times; ch 1. Join. *Rnd 3:* Sl st in 2 dc, sl st in sp, ch 3, in same sp make 2 dc, ch 2 and 3 dc; (ch 1, 3 dc in next ch-1 sp, ch 1, in next corner sp make 3 dc, ch 2 and 3 dc) 3 times; ch 1, 3 dc

in last ch-1, sp, ch 1. Join and fasten off.

*Finishing:* Place wrong sides of 2 motifs tog and, starting at center of right-hand corner with self yarn and tapestry needle, sew the 2 center loops (1 loop from each motif) of sts across to center of next corner. Fasten off. Join 11 motifs to form a single strip. Make 16 more single strips. Join strips to form 11×17 motif throw.

*Fringe:* Wind yarn 50 times around a 7″ square. Cut strands at one end, this makes 14″ strands. Fold 4 strands to form a loop. Insert hook in a sp on narrow edge and draw loop through. Draw ends through loop and pull up tightly to form a knot. Knot a 4-strand fringe in each sp along each narrow edge. Trim evenly.

## CROCHETED CHENILLE HAT

MATERIALS: Reynold's Velourette, 1-oz. balls, 2 balls rose; size I crochet hook *or any size hook which will obtain the stitch gauge below.*

GAUGE: 6 sts = 2"; 6 rows = 2".

DIRECTIONS: *Crown:* Ch 4. Join with sl st to form ring. *Rnd 1:* Make 6 sc in ring. Join with sl st to first sc. *Rnd 2:* Ch 1, 2 sc in same sc as joining, 2 sc in each sc around. Join to first sc (total of 12 sc). *Rnd 3:* Ch 1, sc in same sc as joining, * 2 sc in next sc (inc); sc in next sc, rpt from * around, end with 2 sc in last sc. *Rnd 4:* Ch 1, sc in same sc as joining, increasing 6 sc evenly spaced around, sc in each sc. *Rnds 5-10:* Without letting incs fall over incs of previous rnd, rpt Rnd 4 six times—60 sc. *Rnds 11-26:* Ch 1, sc in each sc around. *Brim—Rnd 1:* Rpt Rnd 4 of Crown, *Rnd 2:* Ch 1, sc in same sc as joining, sc in each sc. Join. *Rnds 3-10:* Rpt last 2 rnds. *Rnds 11-13:* Work 3 rnds even. Break off and fasten. *Ribbon:* Working double strands, ch 160. End off. At 1½" intervals, weave ribbon in and out of hat, right above junction of brim and crown. Tie into large bow.

# For the Men in Your Life

## AUDIO RACKS

MATERIALS: Miter box; white glue; ¾" wire nails; clear shellac; ⅜" thick lattice as follows: CASSETTE TRAY: 21 feet of 1⅛"; TAPE BIN: 13 feet of 1⅜" and 14 feet of 1⅛"; RECORD RACK: 32 feet of 1⅝".

## CASSETTE TRAY

*(about 11"×12")*

DIRECTIONS:

1. Cut 1⅛" lattice as follows: Four 13½" Sides, four 11¼" Ends, four 11¼" Bottoms, four 10¾" Dividers and eight 3½" Corner strips. Use miter box to assure that ends of each piece are cut square with sides.

2. Glue and nail the cut edges of two Sides to the inside edge of two Ends to make top frame.

3. To make bottom frame, repeat top frame. With bottom frame upside down, lay a Bottom strip flat across frame at each end, edges flush. Glue and nail. Three inches inside each Bottom strip, glue and nail two more Bottom strips (3½" from each other) ends flush with sides.

4. With top frame upside down on a work surface, glue Corner strips upright to each side flush with work surface and frame ends. Glue remaining Corner strips to ends of frame flush with side Corner strips. Trim nails to about ⅜" and nail corners, starting the holes with an untrimmed nail.

5. Lay scraps of lattice across corners to establish the space between the two frames. Then place bottom frame upside down on the scraps and glue to corners. Nail to corners with trimmed nails.

*Color photo on page 74*

6. Turn rack right side up and remove lattice scraps. Center a Divider across each Bottom strip gluing ends and bottom edge. Nail at each end. Above this, glue and nail ends of another Divider to the sides flush with top of frame.

7. Finish with clear shellac.

## TAPE BIN
*(about 12″×13″)*

DIRECTIONS:

1. Cut 1⅜″ lattice as follows: Four 12½″ Sides, four 12″ Ends, two 11½″ Dividers and four 4″ Corners. Cut 1⅛″ lattice as follows: Two 12½″ Sides, two 12″ Ends, four 12″ Bottoms, two 11½″ Dividers and four 4″ Corners. Use miter box to assure that ends of each piece are cut square with sides.

2. Following Step 2 for Cassette Tray, make top frame out of 1⅜″ lattice and middle frame out of 1⅛″ lattice.

3. Following Step 3 for Cassette Tray, make bottom frame of 1⅜″ lattice, gluing inside Bottom strips only 2¾″ inside the outside Bottom strips.

## RECORD RACK
*(about 13″×16″)*

DIRECTIONS:

1. Cut 1⅝″ lattice as follows: Six 16″ Sides, two 16″ Bottoms, eight 12″ Corner strips, six 12½″ Dividers and six 12½″ Ends. Use miter box to assure that ends of each piece are cut square with sides.

2. Glue and nail the cut edges of two Ends to the inside edge of two Sides to make top frame. Measure and mark Sides 5″ from inside of each End strip. Glue a Divider along each of these marks (dividers should be 5″

apart) and nail twice.

3. Make middle frame same as top frame.

4. To make bottom frame repeat top frame; then, with bottom frame upside down, lay a Bottom strip flat on frame at each side, edges flush. Glue and nail.

5. With top frame upside down on work surface, glue Corner strips upright to each end flush with work surface and frame sides. Glue remaining Corner strips to sides of frame flush with side Corner strips. Trim nails to about ⅜″ and nail twice to each corner, starting the holes with an untrimmed nail.

6. Measure and mark corners 3½″ above first frame. Place lower edge of middle frame at marks; glue and nail (twice) to each corner with trimmed nails.

7. Place bottom frame upside down at top, bottom surface flush with cut ends of corners. Glue and nail twice with trimmed nails.

8. Turn rack right side up. Finish with clear shellac.

## CORK COVERED BOXES
For the ultimate in gift boxes, cover a selection of the plainest-Jane boxes and tins into handsome gift boxes with self-adhesive cork paper.

## OPEN FILE

MATERIALS: $^5/_{16}$″ dowel, 112″; $^5/_{8}$″ dowel, 72″, 1″ dowel, 24″; grey enamel; yellow enamel; red enamel; drill with $^5/_{16}$″ bit; wood glue; ruler.

DIRECTIONS:

1. Cut $^5/_{16}$″ dowel into 16 pieces, each 7″ long; cut $^5/_{8}$″ dowel into eight pieces, each 9″ long; cut 1″ dowel into two pieces, each 12″ long.

2. Paint 1″ and $^5/_{16}$″ dowel pieces grey. Mix small amounts of red enamel with yellow enamel to produce eight graduated shades, painting each $^5/_{8}$″ piece of dowel a different shade as you add more red to the yellow. Let dry.

3. Mark each $^5/_{8}$″ dowel section $^1/_2$″ from each end, with marks in direct line with each other. Drill $^1/_4$″ into dowels at each mark.

4. Place a ruler straight along one 1″ dowel. Mark dowel $^3/_4$″ from each end, and at 1½″ intervals between end marks. Drill $^1/_4$″ into dowel at each mark. Repeat with second 1″ dowel piece.

5. Dab ends of $^5/_{16}$″ dowel pieces with glue. Using photo as a guide, construct file by slipping ends of $^5/_{16}$″ dowel pieces into drilled holes.

## MAN'S HANG-UP TOILET KIT

MATERIALS: ⅜ yd. water-repellent fabric for inside base; ½ yd. lengthwise striped fabric for outside base; 12″×34″ piece of batting; one package ½″ bias tape; 9″ zipper; 12″ elastic, ⅜″ wide; ½″ buckle.

DIRECTIONS: Make paper patterns for base and two pockets, following diagram. Cut base from outside and inside fabric and from a double layer of batting; cut two pockets in inside fabric; cut two strips of outside fabric 7½″×1½″ and 5″×1½″ for straps.

*Sewing:*

1. Turn under edges and ends of straps ¼″. Fold in half lengthwise right sides out. Edgestitch.

2. Quilt outside base to batting on stripes.

3. Stitch long strip to outside, centered, 5″ from bottom edge. Sew buckle to one end of short strap. Stitch other end, centered, 2½″ from top.

4. *Zipper pocket*: Draw 9″ center line as show in diagram. Slash, clipping to corners ½″ from each end. Fold under edges ¼″; place over zipper and edgestitch. Turn under pocket top ½″. Pin pocket to inside base, with bottom and side edges matching. Edgestitch.

5. *Elastic pocket*: Turn under top ¼″ and again ½″ to form casing. Stitch. Turn under bottom ½″. Make pleats at bottom edges to form three 4″ pockets (*see diagram*). Leave ¼″ free at side edges by making pleat only ¾″. Position on inside base 1½″ above lower

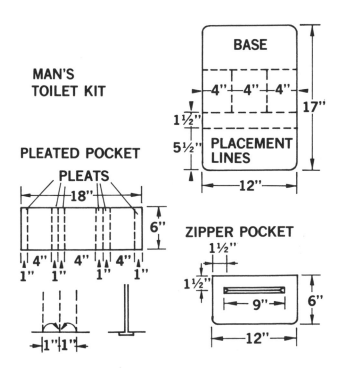

pocket. Edgestitch across bottom, securing pleats. Pull 12″ of elastic through casing. Edgestitch sides in place, catching elastic but leaving pleat free. Distribute gathers evenly and topstitch between pleats from top to bottom to form pockets.

6. Stitch inside base to quilted base, right sides out. Bind stitched edges with bias tape.

## EGG-SHAPED ROPE PLANTER
MATERIALS: One pointed half of a plastic egg-shaped hosiery container; natural-colored wrapping twine; white all-purpose glue; nail.

DIRECTIONS: Using a heated nail, make a small hole, just below the rim of the container. Repeat on opposite side. To make handle, braid a length of twine approximately 2 feet long and insert ends through holes in the egg and knot on the inside. Wrap more twine tightly around the outer surface of the egg, gluing it as you wrap. Start from the bottom point of the egg and work in circles up to the rim.

## TWINE-COVERED PLANTER
MATERIALS: One 4-pack plastic hosiery container; 9½ yards thick coarse twine;

white glue; plastic cement.

DIRECTIONS: Start from rim and wrap twine around outer surface of container, applying plastic cement to rope as you wrap. Make a handle from twine by gluing (with white glue) two 3-foot lengths to bottom of one side of the container and up and over to the opposite side; glue down; let dry. When dry, knot hanger loosely in middle, if desired.

## ROUND SHOELACE PLANTER
MATERIALS: One large 4-pack hosiery container; flat-type shoelaces in colors of your choice; clothesline for handle; white glue or household cement.

DIRECTIONS: Wrap and coil shoelaces in free-form designs; glue to container, pressing firmly as you work. Cut three lengths of clothesline to desired length, for handles. Knot one end of each length and glue to sides of container. Let dry. Make one loop at top by curving ends down and securing with shoelaces wrapped around and glued. Wrap and glue more shoelaces around each cord for decoration.

**WINDOW BOX PLANTER**

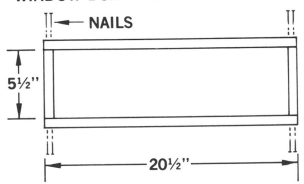

## WINDOW BOX PLANTER

MATERIALS: 6 feet of ⅝"×6" common pine; 16 feet of 1½" wide lattice stripping; 6d finishing nails; hammer; saw; ruler; fine and coarse sandpaper; white glue; wood sealer (we used WaterLox); wood stain and varnish or wax; paint brush.

DIRECTIONS: Cut pine into two 5½" pieces and two 20½" pieces for sides, one 19½" piece for bottom. Smooth ends of all box pieces with coarse sandpaper. If you wish to plant directly in box, give each piece 2 coats of wood sealer to guard against rotting. To construct a box, fasten sides with two 6d nails at each corner, as shown in diagram. Insert bottom, checking fit. Glue and nail flush to bottom edge using three 6d nails each side. (*Note*: When working with glue, be sure to use thin, even coats. Wipe away excess glue with a wet rag before it dries, to avoid spotting wood surface.) Sand edges and corners

with fine sandpaper. *To trim:* Cut lattice into eight 2½" pieces, four 6½" pieces and four 20½" pieces. Trim short sides first by gluing 6½" pieces along top and bottom edges, and 2½" pieces along side edges (trim will form a rectangle). Weight down and let dry (about 2 hours). Repeat on other short side. Trim one long side (20½" pieces on top and bottom edges, 2½" pieces on side edges). Weight down and let dry. Repeat for other long side. When box is completely dry, sand all surfaces with fine sandpaper and fill in any gaps with white glue. Stain box. To finish surface and waterproof box, apply 2 or 3 coats of wax, varnish or wood sealer.

## TENNIS RACQUET COVER
## AND TOTE BAG
### RACQUET COVER

MATERIALS: ½ yard 36" wide heavy cotton fabric in a dark solid; ¼ yard each 36" wide heavy cotton fabric in medium and light solids; 2 yards ½" wide bias tape (to match medium fabric); thread to match bias tape; contrasting threads for appliqués; 12" metal neck zipper to match bias tape; scissors; ¼ yard fusible webbing (18" wide); paper for patterns; compass or suitable round object.

DIRECTIONS: *In dark fabric:* Following directions on page 140, enlarge pattern and trace onto paper. Cut out pattern pieces. Using pattern, cut 2 cover pieces. Mark appliqué positions on right side of one piece. Cut a rectangle 2½"×3", and a circle 6" in diameter; cut circle in half. *In medium fabric:* Cut a circle 4" in diameter; cut circle in half. *In light fabric:* Cut a stripe, 2"×11". Cut pieces of fusible webbing to match sizes and shapes of all but cover pieces. Match webbing pieces to wrong sides of appliqués; pin together. Referring to diagram, arrange design on cover piece over marks. Pin down appliqués to prevent slipping. Following manufacturer's directions for webbing, iron down appliqués. *To machine appliqué:* Use zigzag satin-type stitch. (Stitch setting should be on highest width number, and closest length number.) Be sure to pull fabric along to prevent bunching. Sew circles down with light thread; sew stripe down with brighter contrasting thread. *To make loop:* Fold 2½"×3" rectangle of dark fabric in half lengthwise, right sides together. Seam ⅛" from both long edges. Turn right side out; press, then topstitch ⅛″ in on both sides. Fold under ¼″ on each short end. Pin on appliquéd cover front 1¼″ up from base. Stitch down on short ends, moving back and forth for reinforcement. *To attach zipper:* With zipper closing toward base of cover, baste the wrong side of the zipper closing to wrong sides of front and back. Diagram shows a front view of this procedure. Take a 13″ piece of bias tape and slip over basted zipper on cover back, folding tape in half over edge to form binding. Topstitch down, using thread to match tape. Pin wrong sides of cover front and back together, pinching zipper end slightly to ease into seam where cover pieces are joined. Fold bias tape over pinned seam all the way around cover, forming binding; pin down. Topstitch over tape. *To finish bottom:* Cut a 6″ piece bias tape. Match center of tape to side seam; fold tape over bottom edge and topstitch down, leaving 1″ overlap at each end of zipper opening. Fold ends inside cover and under zipper; tack down by hand.

*Color photo on page 74*

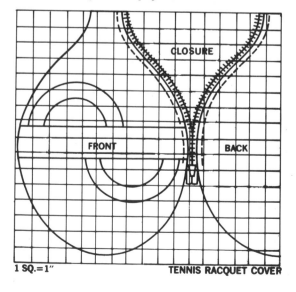

1 SQ.=1″          **TENNIS RACQUET COVER**

## TOTE BAG

**MATERIALS:** Heavy cotton fabrics to match those on racquet cover: ⅓ yard dark, ⅙ yard each medium and light solids; threads (same as on cover); scissors; compass; pins; ⅙ yard fusible webbing (18″ wide); two 1 yard lengths nylon cord (to match color of fabrics used); safety pin.

**DIRECTIONS:** *In dark fabric:* Cut rectangle 8″×24″; cut 2 circles 2″ in diameter; cut circles in half. *In medium fabric:* Cut 2 circles 4″ in diameter; cut circles in half. *In light fabric:* Cut 2 stripes, 1¼″×8″. Cut pieces of fusible webbing to match all pieces but 8″×24″ rectangle. Pin webbing pieces to wrong sides of appliqués. Arrange and pin down design on right side of 8″×24″ fabric (place tops of horizontal stripes 5¾″ from each short end; place circles ¾″ in from long edges). Following manufacturer's directions for webbing, iron appliqués to fabric. Machine appliqué pieces, as on racquet cover. *To form bag:* Press short ends under (to wrong side) ¼″ and stitch ⅛″ in from tops. On wrong sides, mark a point 2″ down from each short end. Fold rectangle in half lengthwise, right sides together, matching stripes; pin side seams. Stitch, leaving ⅜″ seam on each side, beginning at the 2″ mark. Turn right side out; iron, pressing down ⅜″ seam allowance on 2″ unstitched seam. Stitch down pressed seam allowance ¼″ in from side edges. Fold 2″ remainders in half to form casing; pin; topstitch ¾″ from top, reinforcing at each end. *To insert drawstrings:* Using safety pin, draw both cords (one at a time) through casing in opposite directions. Knot ends of each cord (to form two cord loops).

## MEN'S SOCKS

Directions are given for Men's Size Small (10-10½). Changes for Medium (11-11½) and Large (12-12½) are in parentheses.

**MATERIALS:** One 4 oz. skein 4 ply multicolor blue wool or acrylic (A); one 4 oz. skein 4 ply gold wool or acrylic (B); dp needles, 1 set Size 5, *or any size needles which will obtain stitch guage below.*

**GAUGE:** 5 sts = 1″; 7 rows = 1″.

**DIRECTIONS:**

*CUFF AND LEG:* With color B, cast on 44 (48, 52) sts—16 (16, 16) on each of 2 needles, and 12 (16, 20) sts on 3rd needle. Join, being careful not to twist sts. Work k 2, p 2 ribbing

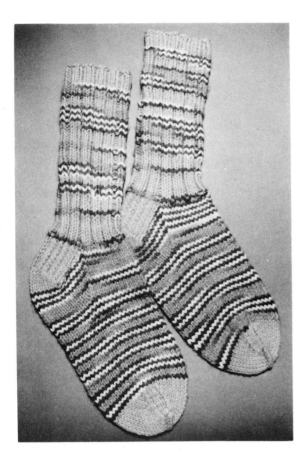

in pattern as follows: 7 rows of B; 5 rows of A; 3 rows of B; 8 rows of A; 5 rows of B; 2 rows of A; 3 rows of B; 7 rows of A; 2 rows of B; 4 rows of A; 4 rows of B; 2 rows of A; 7 rows of B; 2 rows of A, until work measures 8″. *Next Row:* Sl 16 sts of 1st needle and 4 (6, 6) sts of 2nd needle onto one needle (heel); sl rem 24 (26, 30) sts onto stitch holder (instep).

*HEEL:* With B, k 1 row; p 1 row. *Row 1:* K 1, sl 1, rpt to end. *Row 2:* P to end. Rpt these 2 rows 9 (10, 10) more times for 18 (20, 20) rows. *Heel Turn:* On last p row, p only 14 (15, 15) sts of the 20 (22, 22) sts; turn. *Row 1:* Sl 1, k 6, sl 1, psso, k 1; turn. *Row 2:* Sl 1, p 7, p 2 tog, p 1; turn. *Row 3:* Sl 1, k 8, sl 1, k 1, psso, k 1; turn. *Row 4:* Sl 1, p 9, p 2 tog, p 1, turn. *Row 5:* Sl 1, k 10, sl 1, k 1, psso, k1; turn. *Row 6:* Sl 1, p 11, p 2 tog, p 1. There should be 14 (16, 16) sts left.

*GUSSETS AND FOOT:* With A, pick up and k 10 (11, 11) sts on side of heel, k 7 (8, 8) sts of heel onto 1st needle; k 7 (8, 8) sts of heel onto 2nd needle; pick up and k 10 (11, 11) sts on other side of heel; k 24 (26, 30) sts from holder onto 3rd needle. There will be 17 (19, 19) sts on 1st and 2nd needles and 24 (26, 30) sts on

3rd. *Dec Row:* k 1, sl 1, k 1, psso, k 14 (16, 16) sts onto 1st needle; k 14 (16, 16) sts, k 2 tog, k 1 on 2nd needle; k 1, sl 1, k 1, psso, k 18 (20, 24), k 2 tog, k 1 on 3rd needle; rpt this dec row every other row 7 times until there are 10 (11, 11) sts on 1st and 2nd needles (heel) and 24 (26, 30) sts on 3rd needle (instep). Continue knitting until sock measures 7 (8, 9)″ from heel or 2″ less than length of foot.

*TOE:* With B, beg at center of sole, k to within 3 sts of end of 1st needle, k 2 tog, k 1; on 2nd needle k 1, sl 1, k 1, psso, k to last 3 sts, k 2 tog, k 1; on 3rd needle, k 1, sl 1, psso, k to end of needle. *Row 2:* k row. *Row 3:* K 1st needle; on 2nd needle, k 1, sl 1, k 1, psso, k to last 3 sts, k 2 tog, k 1; k 3rd needle. *Row 4:* K row. *Row 5:* Rpt row 1. *Row 6:* k. *Row 7:* Rpt row 3. *Row 8:* K. Rpt rows 1 and 2 until 16 (20, 20) sts rem. There will be 4 (5, 5) sts on 1st and 3rd needles and 8 (10, 10) sts on 2nd needle. K 4 (5, 5) sts on 1st needle onto 3rd needle and k to end of needle. *To Finish:* Cut yarn, leaving a 16″ length; thread a tapestry needle and weave sts from sole and instep tog until all sts are joined.

**MAN'S BELT—CLOTHESLINE CRAFTS**
Directions are for 35″ belt. Adjust clothesline lengths for desired size, remembering that there are 4 coils of clothesline to adjust for extra length.
MATERIALS: Tapestry needle; 12 feet of ¼″-diameter clothesline or rope; double-ply wool yarn in the following colors and amounts: 23 yards dark brown, 10 yards blue, 2 yards pale green, 32 yards tan; wooden button. *Note:* Select button to fit loop after you've completed belt.
DIRECTIONS: Following General Directions for basic wrap technique on page 85 and how to change colors, wrap 4½″ of clothesline with dark brown yarn. Changing to blue yarn, wrap 1″; change back to dark brown yarn and wrap 2½″ to 3″. Repeat pattern; make eight 1″ blue bands. (For smaller belts, make 7 blue bands; for larger belts, make 9.) After last blue band, wrap 6″ with dark brown; wrap, then shape a loop approximately 1″ long to form button-hole *(see diagram)*; attach 2 coils of clothesline to each other by wrapping yarn 5 or 6 times around both pieces of clothesline. Continue wrapping and stitching 2 coils of clothesline to each other; before each

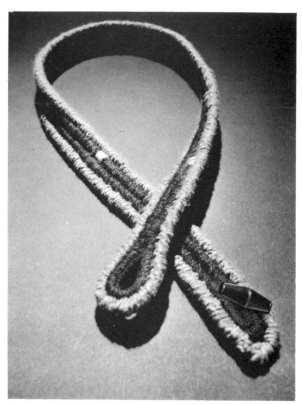

**MAN'S BELT**

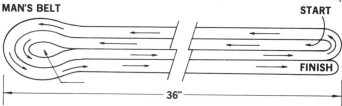

START

FINISH

— 36" —

blue band on the first length of clothesline, change to blue yarn, wrap 1½". Complete second length of clothesline with dark brown yarn, wrapping and stitching until it is as long as the first length. Using pale green yarn, wrap 3 times (over wrapped clothesline) in center of each blue band on the second length of clothesline. Change to tan yarn; bend clothesline around end of first length (as shown in diagram). Wrap and stitch with tan yarn around entire belt; cut clothesline off at end of fourth length. Try on belt; sew button where desired.

## HAT AND SCARF SET

Scarf measures 10″×50″, excluding fringe. Directions are given for hat which fits all sizes.

MATERIALS: Coats & Clark's Red Heart "Wintuk" 4 Ply, (3½ oz. "Tangleproof" Pull

Out Skeins): Blue. For scarf: 2 skeins; for hat: 1 skein AND Coats and Clark's Red Heart "Wintuk" Sport Yarn, 2 Ply (2 oz. "Tangleproof" Pull Out Skeins): Royal Blue. For scarf: 2 skeins; for hat: 1 skein; 1 pair No. 10½ knitting needles, or any size needles which will obtain the stitch gauge; crochet hook for scarf; darning needle for hat.

GAUGE: Slightly stretched: On No. 10½ needles: 4 sts = 1″; 9 rows = 2″. *Important:* Use 1 strand each of Blues and Royal Blue held together throughout knitting of scarf.

DIRECTIONS: Starting at one narrow edge, with 1 strand each of Blues and Royal Blue held together and No. 10½ needles, cast on 42 sts. *Row 1 (wrong side):* P 2,* k2, p 2. Rpt from * across. *Row 2:* K2, * p 2, k 2. Rpt from * across. Rpt Rows 1 and 2 alternately for rib pattern. Work in rib pat until total length is about 50″, end with Row 1. Bind off in ribbing. *Fringe:* With 1 strand each of Blues and Royal Blue held together, wind yarn around a 4½″ square of cardboard; cut loops open at one edge, making 9″ strands. (Cut strands as you go along attaching them to scarf to determine amount needed). Hold 2 strands of each color together and fold in half to form a loop. With right side of scarf facing up, insert crochet hook from back to front through center of first rib at beg of one narrow edge of scarf and draw looped strands through. Draw loose ends through loop with crochet hook; pull ends tightly to form a knot. Tie one group of 2 strands of each color in same way in center of each rib across narrow edge. Tie

*Color photo on page 74*

fringe onto other short end in the same way. Trim all fringe evenly. To finish, lay scarf flat on a soft towel; steam very lightly.

HAT

DIRECTIONS: Starting at outer edge of cuff, with 1 strand each of Blues and Royal Blue held together and No. 10½ needles, cast on 76 sts. *Row 1:* Work in k 2, p 2 ribbing across. Mark this row for wrong side. Work in ribbing as established until total length is 13", end with a row on wrong side. *Next Row:* * K 2, p 2 together, Rpt from * across. *Following Row:* * K 1, p 2 together. Rpt from * across. *Next Row:* K 2 together across. Break off, leaving a 20" length of yarn. Thread this end into a darning needle and draw through remaining sts, pull up tightly and fasten securely. Sew back seam to within 4½" from lower edge; then reverse seam for cuff. Lay hat flat on a soft towel; steam very lightly. Fold about 4½" to right side to form cuff.

# Boys and Girls

*Color photo on page 76*

## RAINBOW SNEAKERS

Use thick applications of fabric paint to make rainbow sneakers. When dry, heat-set in 200° oven for 10 minutes.

*Color photo on page 76*

## LAVENDER AND OLD LACE SNEAKERS

Your baby girl will love these sneakers: Dye with pink/orchid. Dry; glue on lace medallion and trim around rubber.

*Color photo on page 75*

## PINK PONY PAJAMA BAG

MATERIALS: 1 yd. pink print fabric; ½ yd. heavyweight interfacing; ¼ yd. pink felt; Wright's medium brite pink rickrack; 1¾ yds. Wright's lace and tape combo (pink); 1 yd. Wright's 3" orlon fringe; 2 small black pompons from Wright's ball fringe; 14" Wright's pink zipper; fiberfill stuffing; scissors; pencil; paper for pattern; straight pins.

DIRECTIONS: Following directions on page 140, enlarge and cut out patterns. From pink print fabric, cut out two rocking horses, one back gusset, one front gusset, one bottom (23"×5½") and one inside pajama pocket (14"×22"). Sew horse front to horse back from A to B, using ½" seam (see diagram). Pin and sew in back gusset, matching at A. Cut three pieces of interfacing the same size as the bottom piece (23"×5½"). Pin and sew

**PAJAMA BAG**     1 SQ. = 2"

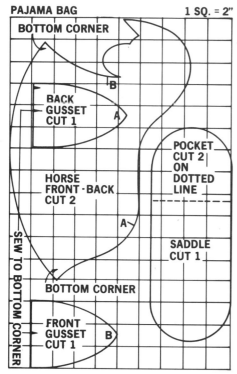

three pieces of interfacing to the wrong side of bottom piece. With right sides together, sew one side of bottom to the bottom of the horse. Sew the other side of bottom piece to the bottom of the horse, leaving a 14″ opening for zipper. Baste in the zipper, turning under raw edges. Fold pocket in half (now 14″×11″) and sew sides closed. Put the pajama pocket in place inside the horse, turn under raw edges and baste to inside of zipper. Sew pocket, zipper and horse bottom together. Zipper should open to reveal inside pajama pocket. With right sides together, pin and sew in front gusset, matching at B. Leave an opening to stuff. Clip all curves, turn to right side and stuff. (Stuff body loosely to allow room for pajamas.) Sew front gusset closed. Cut pink rickrack in half and interlock the two pieces to make bridle and reins. Sew in place as shown. Sew on two black pompons for eyes, as shown. Cut two 11″ pieces of white fringe and sew together where fringe starts. Open top and sew fringe bands in place for mane. Cut two 6″ pieces of fringe and sew together where fringe starts. Sew one end of fringe to the horse for a tail, as shown. Cut pink felt "saddle" and two slipper pockets. Trim pocket tops with lace. Sew pockets on both ends of "saddle" and add trim as shown.

## SHERPA SLIPPERS

*(age 7 to 11)*

MATERIALS *(for one pair):* ⅛ yd. 40″ lining and 60″ Sherpa or scraps of both; purchased appliqué; washable knitting worsted.

DIRECTIONS: Following directions on page 140, enlarge pattern and cut out. Cut one top and one sole for each slipper from Sherpa and lining.

*Sewing:* 1. With right sides together, stitch each Sherpa to a matching lining piece, leaving a 3″ opening. 2. Trim Sherpa seam allowances; clip curves. Turn and slip stitch opening. Press. 3. Buttonhole stitch around all edges (*see* BASIC EMBROIDERY STITCHES). Crochet to connect pieces as follows.

MATERIALS FOR CROCHET: Knitting Worsted 4 Ply (4 oz. skeins): 1 skein of desired color for each garment; crochet hook, size I, *or any size hook which will obtain the stitch gauge;* a large darning needle.

GAUGE: 7 sc = 2″.

*Crochet Edging:* With right side facing, working in top loops of embroidery sts, sc evenly along entire outer edge of each piece,

**HALF PATTERNS**

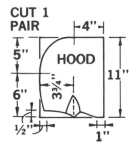

having 7 sc to 2″ (work 1 or 2 sc in each st as needed to keep edges flat), make 3 sc in same st at each corner. Be very careful to have same number of sc along corresponding edges on same piece and along corresponding edges of adjacent pieces to be joined tog, counting from center st of corner to center st of next corner. At end of rnd, join with sl st to first sc. Break off; fasten.

*Joining:* Baste all edges to be joined loosely together. With a large eyed darning needle and same yarn, from right side, working through back loop only of each st, overcast edges together from corner to corner, matching sts. Overcast all seams in same manner.

4. Slipstitch appliqué to center fronts of slippers.

## HOODED SHERPA CARDIGAN

MATERIALS: ¾ yd. each of 45″-wide washable lining and 60″ Sherpa; 1 skein washable 4-ply wool yarn.

DIRECTIONS: Make paper pattern for front,

**SHERPA CARDIGAN**

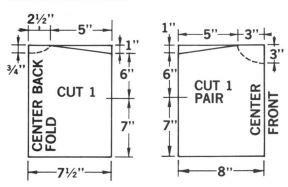

*Color photo on page 75*

back and hood, following diagram. Sleeve is 11″ square. Hood dart is 3¾″ high, 1″ wide at base and starts ½″ above base of diagram.

*Cutting:* Cut one back, two sleeves, a pair of fronts (one left, one right) and a pair of hoods from both Sherpa and lining.

*Sewing:* Line and join pieces (including hood darts and underarm seams), following Steps 1 to 3 for Sherpa Slippers leaving a 6″ opening. Crochet drawstring for hood.

## STRIPED STOCKING CAP AND MITTENS

Directions for set are given for size Small (2–4 years). Changes for sizes Medium (6–8 years) and Large (10–12 years) are in parentheses.

MATERIALS: Rochelle Dazzle, 4 Ply (4 oz. skeins): 1 skein each of Snow White (A), Bright Pink (B) and Grass Green (C); crochet hooks, Sizes J and H, *or any size hook which*

*will obtain the stitch gauge below.*
Gauge:   Cap—7 sc = 2″; 7 rows = 2″.
                Mittens—4 sc = 1″; 4 rows = 1″.

MEASUREMENT AROUND PALM OF MITTEN:

| SMALL | MEDIUM | LARGE |
|---|---|---|
| 4-4½″ | 5-5½″ | 6-6½″ |

*Stocking Cap:* Starting at end of scarf with A and Size J hook, ch 4. Join with sl st to form ring. *Rnd 1*: 8 sc in ring. Do not join rnds, but mark beg of each rnd. *Rnd 2*: * Sc in next sc, 2 sc in next sc—*inc made*; rpt from * around—12 sc. *Rnd 3*: * Sc in each of next 2 sc, 2 sc in next sc; rpt from * around—4 incs made. Drop A to wrong side; pick up B and draw a loop through loop on hook, pull dropped strand tightly—*color change made.* *Rnd 4*: With B, * sc in each of next 3 sc, 2 sc in next sc; rpt from * around—20 sc. *Rnd 5*: Being careful not to have incs fall directly above incs of previous rnd, sc in each sc, making 4 incs evenly spaced around. *Rnd 6*: Rpt Rnd 5—28 sc. Drop B; pick up C and draw a loop through loop on hook, pull dropped strand tightly. Hereafter always make color change in this manner; do not break off colors not in use, carry strands loosely on wrong side of work. *Rnds 7 and 8*: With C, work same as for Rnd 5—36 sc in last rnd. *Rnd 9*: With C, sc in each sc around. Change to A. Now, working same as for Rnd 9, continue to make 3 rnds A, 3 rnds B and 3 rnds C for Stripe pat until total length is about 30″ from beg, ending with a complete stripe.

*Shaping For Cap:* Mark last rnd made. Continuing in Stripe pat throughout, inc 4 sc evenly spaced on every other rnd until there are 56 (60, 64) sc in rnd. Work even, making sc in each sc over these sts until length from marked rnd is approximately 7(7½, 8)″, ending with a complete stripe. At end of last rnd, sl st in each of next 3 sc. Break off all colors and fasten. Darn in any loose ends on wrong side.

*Pompon:* Cut 2 cardboard circles, each 3″ in diameter. Cut a hole 1½″ in diameter at center of each circle. Cut 2 strands each of B and C, each 8 yards long. Place cardboard circles tog and holding 4 strands (2 strands of each color) together, wind yarn around the double circle, drawing yarn through center opening

*Color photo on page 76*

and over edge until center hole is filled. Cut yarn around outer edge between cardboards. Double a separate strand of yarn and slip between cardboard circles, tie securely around strands of pompon. Remove cardboard and trim evenly. Tack to starting ring at beg of scarf. Fold up cuff to right side at lower edge of cap.

*Right Mitten: Back—Row 1*: Starting at center with C and Size H hook, ch 15(17, 19), sc in 2nd ch from hook, sc in each ch to last ch, 3 sc in last ch—*top edge;* working along opposite side of starting chain, sc in each of next 13(15, 17) ch—29(33, 37) sc. Ch 1, turn. *Row 2*: Sc in each sc to within 3-sc group, 2 sc in each of next 3 sc, sc in each rem sc—32(36,40) sc. Break off C. Pick up B and ch 1, turn. *Row 3*: With B, sc in each of first 15(17,19) sc, 2 sc in each of next 3 sc—*3 incs made at top edge;* sc in each rem sc. Ch 1, turn. *Row 4*: Sc in each sc to within center 5 sc at top edge, 2 sc in next sc, sc in each of next 3 sc, 2 sc in next sc, sc in each rem sc—37(41,45) sc. Ch 1, turn. Rpt last row 0(1,1) more time—37(43,47) sc. Ch 1, turn. *Next Row (Thumb Row)*: Sc in each sc to center 5 sc at top edge, 2 sc in next sc, sc in each of next 3 sc, 2 sc in next sc, sc in each of next 9(11,13) sc; ch 7(8,9) for Thumb, sc in 2nd ch from hook, sc in each of next 5(6,7) ch, sc in same sc as last sc made before thumb chain, sc in each of rem 7(8,9) sc. Ch 1, turn. *Next Row:* Sc in each sc to tip of thumb, 3 sc in sc at tip of thumb, working along opposite side of chain, sc (hdc, dc) in each ch st of thumb, sc in each sc to end of row. Break; fasten.

*Front:* Work same as for Back until 3(4,4) rows have been completed—35(41,45) sc. Ch 1, turn. *Next Row (Thumb Row):* Sc in each of first 16(18,20) sc, 2 sc in next sc, sc in next 1(3,3) sc, 2 sc in next sc, sc in each of next 10(11,12) sc; ch 7(8,9) for Thumb, sc in 2nd ch from hook, sc in next 5(6,7) ch, sc in same sc as last sc made before thumb chain, sc in each rem sc. Ch 1, turn. *Next Row:* Work same as last row of Back. Break off and fasten.

With a darning needle and C, matching edges, (easing in top edge of back to fit) sew back and front tog, leaving lower edge open. *Cuff—Rnd 1:* Working along lower edge over ends of rows, attach A to end of seam, sc evenly along entire lower edge, being careful to keep work flat. Join with sl st to first sc. *Rnd 2:* Ch 1, sc in same sc as joining, sc in each sc around. Join to first sc. Rpt last row 2(3,4) more times. Break off and fasten. *Left Mitten:* Work to correspond with Right Mitten, reversing position of Thumb.

Steam cap and mittens very lightly through a damp cloth; do not press.

## CHILD'S BOATNECK PULLOVER

Directions are given for size 2. Changes for size 4, 6, and 8 are in parentheses,
MATERIALS: Coats & Clark's O.N.T. Speed Cro-Sheen: 2 (3,4,4) balls each of white and Spanish Red; knitting needles, 1 pair each of No. 3 and No. 5, or any size needles which will obtain the stitch gauge.
GAUGE: 11 sts = 2"; 7 rows = 1".

MEASUREMENTS:

| SIZES: | 2 | 4 | 6 | 8 |
|---|---|---|---|---|
| BODY CHEST SIZE: | 21" | 23" | 24" | 26" |
| CHEST: | 22" | 24" | 25" | 27" |

*Back:* Starting at inner edge of hem with Red and No. 3 needles, cast on 61 (67,69,75) sts. Work in st st (k 1 row, p 1 row) for 5 rows for hem, ending with a k row. From wrong side, working in back of each st, k next row for hemline. Change to No. 5 needles and work in Stripe pattern as follows: Attach White.

*Rows 1 through 4:* With Red, starting with a k row, work in st st. Drop Red; pick up White *Note: Carry color not in use loosely along side edge of work. Rows 5 through 8:* With White, work in st st. Rpt these 8 rows (Rows 1 through 8) for Stripe pattern until total length is 8" (8½,9,9½)" from hemline, end with Row 4 or Row 8 of Stripe pattern.

*Armhole Shaping:* Continuing in Stripe pattern throughout, bind off 2 (3,3,4) sts at beg of next 2 rows. Dec. one st at each end every other row 2 (3,3,3) times—53 (55,57,61) sts. Work even (no more decs) until length is about 4" (4½,5,5½)" from first row of armhole shaping, ending with Row 4 or Row 8 of Stripe pattern.

*Shoulder Shaping:* Continuing in Stripe pattern, bind off 5 sts at beg of next 2 rows; 4 (4,5,6) sts at beg of following 2 rows—35 (37,37,39) sts. Change to No. 3 needles. *Next row:* From right side, p across for turning ridge. For facing, starting with a p row, continue in st st with same color used for last stripe, increasing one st at each end every other row twice—39 (41,41,43) sts. Bind off loosely.

*Front:* Work same as Back.
*Sleeves:* Starting at inner edge of hem with Red and No. 3 needles, cast on 47 (49,53,55) sts. Work same as for Back until length is about 3" (3½,3½,4)" from hemline, end with same pattern row as on Back before Armhole Shaping.

*Top Shaping:* Continuing in Stripe pattern,

*Color photo on page 75*

bind off 2 (3,3,4) sts at beg of next 2 rows. Dec one st at each end every other row 2 (4,4,6) times; dec one st at each end every row until 19 sts remain. Bind off 2 sts at beg of next 4 rows. Bind off remaining 11 sts.

*Finishing:* Block to measurements. Sew shoulder seams, including facing. Sew side and sleeve seams, matching stripes. Turn all hems to wrong side at hemline and stitch in place. Turn neck facing on turning ridge to wrong side and stitch in place. Sew in sleeves, matching stripes.

## DAISY SWEATER

Directions are given for size 4. Changes for sizes 6 and 8 are in parentheses.

MATERIALS: Columbia-Minerva Nantuk Sports Yarn (2 oz. pull skeins) 3 (4-4) skeins white yarn (Color A); 1 skein each of green and yellow (Colors B & C); 1 pair each "Boye" knitting needles, sizes 4 and 6; yarn bobbins.

GAUGE: 5 sts = 1"; 13 rows = 2"

DIRECTIONS: *Front:* With Size 4 needles and Color A, cast on 63 (69-73). K 1 row and P 1 row for 5 rows for facing. K next row for turn of hem. Change to Size 6 needles. *Row 1—Right Side:* K 30 (33-35) A; join a B bobbin, K 3 for stem, join a 2nd skein or bobbin of A and K last 30 (33-35). *Row 2:* P 30 (33-35) A, 3 B, 30 (33-35) A. Repeat these 2 rows 10 (12-15) more times.

Breaking and joining colors as needed, fol-

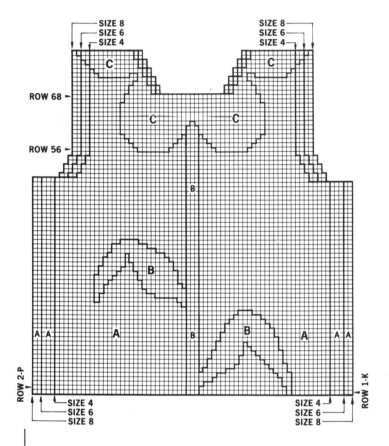

*Color photo on page 76*

low chart*, starting with Row 1. Work to armhole, end on wrong side. Width is 12½ (13½-14½)" and length is about 10 (10½-11½)" above turn.

*Armholes:* Continue to follow chart, bind off 5 (6-6) at beg of next 2 rows. Dec 1 each side on next row then every other row twice more, end on right side: 47 (51-55) sts. Starting with Row 56 of chart, work through Row 68, end on wrong side.

*Neck:* Continuing to follow chart, work 16 (17-18) sts and sl them to a holder, work center 15 (17-19) and sl them to a 2nd holder for neck, work to end. Dec 1 at neck every other row 4 times. Work on rem'ing 12 (13-14) sts to top of chart, end at armhole edge.

*Shoulder:* With Color C, bind off 6 (6-7) at armhole edge once then 6 (7-7) at same edge once. Starting at opposite neck edge, work other side.

*Back:* With Color A, omitting chart, work same as front until armhole shaping has been completed 47 (51-55) sts. Starting on wrong side with Row 56 on chart, finish same as front.

*Sleeves:* With Size 4 needles and Color A, cast

on 32 (34-38). K 1 row and P 1 row for 5 rows. K next row for turn. Change to Size 6 needles. K 1 row and P 1 row for 6 rows. Work in St St, inc'ing 1 each side on the 5th row then every 6th row 7 (7-8) more times. Work on the 48 (50-56) sts to 11 (12-13)″ or desired length above turn. Width is 9½ (10-11)″.

*Neckband:* Sew left shoulder seam. With Size 4 needles and Color C, starting at open shoulder on right side pick up and K 72 (76-80) around neck including holders. K 1 and P 1 in ribbing for 3″. Bind off loosely in ribbing. Sew open shoulder joining neckband. Sew sleeves in place then sew side and sleeve seams. Fold neckband in half and sew to wrong side. Turn in hems and facing and sew to wrong side.

* Wind a separate bobbin for each color change. When changing colors, always pick up next color from *under* dropped color to prevent a hole. Break off and join colors as needed. Any small color section may be covered with Duplicate Stitch (*See* BASIC EMBROIDERY STITCHES).

## GIRL'S CROCHETED SAILOR PINAFORE

Directions are given for size 2. Changes for size 4 are in parentheses.

MATERIALS: Coats & Clark's Knitting Worsted, 4(6) ozs. White (A) and 1(2) ozs. Navy (B); crochet hook Size G, *or any size hook which will obtain the stitch gauge below;* 2 buttons; 2 red star appliqués; white narrow elastic.

GAUGE: 3½ sts = 1″; 4 rows = 1″.

| MEASUREMENTS: | | |
|---|---|---|
| SIZES: | 2 | 4 |
| WAIST BEFORE INSERTING ELASTIC | 24½″ | 26¾″ |

*Bib:* With A, ch 22(26) loosely. *Row 1 (right side):* Work 1 dc in 4th ch from hook (first 3 ch counts as 1 dc) and in each ch across—20(24) dc. Ch 3, turn. *Row 2:* With turning ch as first dc, sk first dc, work 1 dc in each dc across. Ch 3, turn. Rpt Row 2 for 6(10) rows more. Fasten off. *Row 1:* Turn square clockwise and with A work 15(19) sc up side of square, ch 3 in corner to form buttonhole, work 18(22) sc across top of square, ch 3 at corner to form buttonhole, work 15(19) sc down other side of square. Fasten off A. *Row 2:* Attach B at bottom of square where Row 1 was started, work 16(20) sc up side of square, 3 sc in corner, then 20(24) sc across top of square, 3 sc in corner, then work 16(20) sc down other side of square. Fasten off B. *Row 3:* Attach B at bottom of square at starting point, work 1 sc in each sc around 3 sides working 3 sc in each corner. Fasten off B. *Row 4:* Attach A at bottom of square at starting point, work 1 sc in each sc around 3 sides working 2 sc in each corner. Fasten off A.

*Skirt:* Holding bib upside down, with A, work 26(30) sc across bottom of bib, ch 60(64) for back of skirt; join with sl st to first sc, *Rnd 2:* Ch 3, * work 2 dc in next sc, 1 dc in next sc; rpt from * around; join with sl st. *Rnds 3–11 (3–15 for Size 4):* Ch 3, dc in each

dc around; join with sl st. Fasten off.
*Trim: Rnd 1:* Attach B, ch 1, sc in each dc around; join with sl st. *Rnd 2:* Ch 1, sc in each sc around; join with sl st. *Rnd 3:* With A, ch 3, dc in each sc around; join with sl st. *Rnd 4:* With B, ch 1, sc in each dc around; join with sl st. *Rnd 5:* With B, ch 1, sc in each sc around; join with sl st. *Rnd 6:* With A, ch 3, dc in each sc around; join with sl st. Fasten off.
*Sailor Collar Strap:* With A, ch 5. *Row 1:* Work 1 sc in 2nd ch from hook and in each ch across—4 sc. Ch 1, turn. Continue in sc until strap measures 12½(14½)". Fasten off.
*Collar:* Join A at 18th(22nd) row of sc on strap, ch 3, work 15(19) dc along side of strap. Ch 3, turn. *Row 2:* Work dc in each dc of 15(19) dc. Ch 3, turn. Continue in dc for 5(9) rows more to form collar. Fasten off.
*Trim: Row 1:* Join A at 10th(12th) row on side of strap, work about 20(24) sc along strap and up side of collar, work 3 sc in corner, work 15(19) sc along top of collar, work 3 sc in corner, work about 20(24) sc along other side of collar and strap. Ch 1, turn. *Row 2:* With A, work 1 sc in each sc on 3 sides working 3 sc in each corner. Ch 1, turn. (Do not fasten off A.) *Row 3:* Join B at 2nd sc of A, work 19(23) sc or 1 sc less than worked on Row 1 along side of strap and up side of collar, work 3 sc in corner, work 1 sc in each sc along top of collar, work 3 sc in corner, work 19(21) sc or 1 sc less than worked on Row 1 along side of collar and strap. Ch 1, turn. *Row 4:* With B, sc in each sc on 3 sides working 3 sc in each corner. Ch 1, turn. Fasten off. *Row 5:* With A, sc in each sc on 3 sides working 2 sc in each corner; join with sl st. Fasten off.
*Finishing:* Sew a button at end of each strap. Sew a star appliqué in each far corner on collar. Measure waist of child and cut piece of narrow elastic to fit minus measurement of bib on front. Run elastic through top row (ch) of skirt on back and sew it to each side of bib on front.

## TODDLER'S CROCHETED PONCHO

Directions are given for Poncho to fit toddler sizes (1–3 year olds).
MATERIALS: Wintuk Sport Yarn, 2-Ply (2 oz. skeins): 3 skeins Red (A), 1 skein White (B); crochet hook, Size G, *or any size hook which will obtain the stitch gauge below.*
GAUGE: Pattern—3 sts = 1"; 5 rows = 2".

**TODDLER PONCHO JOINING DIAGRAM**

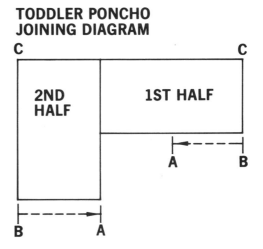

MEASUREMENTS:
(Excluding fringe)
WIDTH ACROSS ENTIRE LOWER EDGE: 54"
LENGTH UP CENTER BACK OR CENTER FRONT: 13"

*Note:* Poncho is worked in two straight pieces, then pieces are joined together.
*First Half:* Starting at outer edge with A, ch 55 to measure 19". *Row 1 (right side):* Sc in 2nd ch from hook, sc in each ch across—54 sc. Ch 1, turn. *Row 2:* Sc in first st, * dc in next st, sc in next st; rpt from * across; ending with dc in last st. Ch 1, turn. *Row 3:* Sc in first dc, * dc in next sc, sc in next dc; rpt from * across, ending with dc in last sc. Ch 1, turn. *Rows 4 through 8:* Rpt Row 3. At end of last row, cut yarn and fasten. Turn. *Row 9:* Attach B to first st on last row, sc in same st, sc in each st across. Ch 1, turn. *Row 10:* Sc in each sc across. Cut yarn and fasten. Turn. *Row 11:* With right side facing, attach A to

first sc, sc in same st, * dc in next st, sc in next st; rpt from * across, ending with dc in last st. *Rows 12 through 16*: Rpt Row 3. At end of last row, cut yarn and fasten. Turn. *Rows 17 through 24*: Rpt Rows 9 through 16; do not cut yarn. Ch 1, turn. *Row 25*: Rpt Row 3 once more. Ch 1, turn. *Row 26*: Sc in each st across. Cut yarn and fasten.

*Second Half:* Work same as First Half.

*Finishing:* Pin each piece to measure approximately 10"×18"; cover with a damp cloth and allow to dry; do not press.

*To Join:* With right sides facing, sew one short edge of first half to first 10" on top edge of second half; sew lower end of second half (A to B) to portion marked A to B on long edge of first half (see diagram). Fold joined pieces matching corners marked C for center back and center front points of poncho.

*Edging:* With right side facing, attach A to end of a seam on outer edge; being careful to keep work flat, sc evenly along entire outer edge of poncho, making 3 sc in same st at each point. Join with sl st to first sc. Cut yarn and fasten.

*Neck Edge: Rnd 1*: Attach A to end of a seam at neck edge, sc in each st along entire neck edge, easing in edge slightly to desired fit. Join with sl st to first sc. *Rnds 2 and 3*: Ch 1, sc in same sc as joining, sc in each sc around. Join with sl st to first sc. *Rnd 4*: Ch 1, working from left to right, sc in next sc to the right, * ch 1, sk next sc, sc in next sc to the right, rpt from * around, ending with ch 1. Join with sl st to first sc. Cut yarn and fasten.

*Pompon: (Make 2)*: Wind B approximately 25 times around a 1" piece of cardboard. Slip loops off cardboard. With a separate double strand tie loops tog at center; cut loops at each end. Trim evenly. With B make chain 1½" long. Cut yarn and fasten. Tack a pompon to each end of chain. Tack center of chain to center front of neck, below edging.

*Fringe:* Wind A 5 times around a 3½" square of cardboard, cut at one edge, making 7" strands. Hold strands together and fold in half to form a loop. With right side facing, insert hook from back to front in any sc on lower edge of poncho and draw loop through; draw loose ends through loop on hook, pull tightly to form a knot. Tie a 5-strand group in same manner in every other st along entire lower edge. Trim evenly.

# Santa's Helpers

## WOODEN TOYS

For these toys, use sanded, varnished dowels ranging from ⅛" to 1½" in diameter. From the overall length and height (*given in that order*), and the dimensions of the main pieces, estimate the size of other pieces. *Rhino and hippo:* 4"×2½"; 1½"×2½" body. *Elephant:* 4"×3; 1½"×2¾" body. *Giraffe,* 7½" tall and *camel,* 3½" tall: 1"×2½" body; ¼" legs. *Gator:* 7½"×1"; ¾"×2" body; ⅝"×3¼" tail. Drill ¾" holes ¼" deep, with the center 1" from each end of each body. In each hole glue ¾"×½" dowel with ¼" hole drilled through. Use photo as guide for assembling.

## WHALE, TURTLE AND FROG

GENERAL MATERIALS: Fabric remnants or scraps in assorted colors and prints; scraps of felt in assorted colors; buttons for eyes; dried beans, aquarium gravel or packaged cat litter for filling.

GENERAL DIRECTIONS: Following directions on page 140, enlarge pattern and cut out number of pieces indicated. Stitch pieces together, with right sides facing, allowing for ⅜" seams.

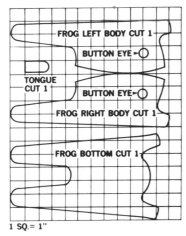

FROG: Cut out frog pieces from fabric indicated on pattern; tongue is cut from a felt scrap. Stitch right sides together along rounded back. Beginning at one side of frog bottom, stitch around legs, attaching frog body to bottom. At center of frog head, insert felt tongue; continue stitching, leaving a 2" opening at side of body. Turn frog right side out; stuff with desired filling. Hand-stitch opening closed. Sew on button eyes.

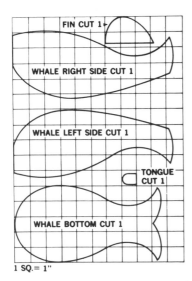

WHALE: Cut out the whale pieces from fabric as indicated on pattern; cut fin and tongue from felt. Stitch left and right sides of whale together along back edge. Insert felt fin at top of head. Beginning at one side near tail, stitch around whale, attaching top to bottom;

insert felt tongue at center of whale head, continue stitching, leaving a 2" opening near tail. Turn whale right side out; stuff with desired filling. Hand-stitch opening closed.

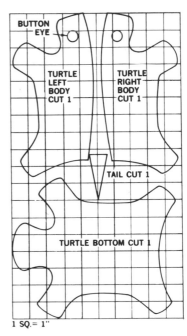

TURTLE: Cut out turtle pieces from fabric as directed in pattern; cut tail from felt scrap. Stitch right and left turtle body together along back edge. Beginning at one side of turtle, stitch around legs, attaching body to bottom; insert felt tail; continue stitching around edge leaving a 2" opening at side of body. Turn turtle right side out; stuff with desired filling. Hand-stitch opening closed. Sew on button eyes as indicated.

*Color photo on page 78*

# HAPPY COW

MATERIALS: Coats & Clark Red Heart® Worsted Sport Yarn, 2 Ply ready-to-use pull-out skns: 6 oz. of Apple Green; 4 oz. each of Amethyst, Yellow, Vibrant Orange and Lt. Pink; scraps of pink, red, yellow and black felt; J. & P. Coats Deluxe Six-Strand Floss, 1 skn of Black; polyester stuffing; crochet hook, Size H or *any size hook which will obtain the stitch gauge below.*
GAUGE: 7 sc = 2″; 4 rows =1″.
(*Note:* Use 2 strands of yarn held together throughout.) Be sure to check your gauge before starting item.
DIRECTIONS: *BODY—Front Hind Section:* With 2 strands of Orange held together, ch 18. *Row 1:* Sc in 2nd ch from hook and in each ch across to last ch, draw up a loop in last ch, drop color in use, with 2 strands of Green yarn over and draw through 2 loops on hook—color change made—17 sc. Break off previous color and fasten. Ch 1, turn. *Always change color in this manner. Row 2:* Sc in each sc across, changing to Orange in last sc. Ch 1, turn. Repeating Row 2 for stitch pattern, work color stripes alternating Orange and Green until 29 rows have been completed, ending with Orange. Break off and fasten.
*Back Hind Section:* Work same as Front Hind Section, working color stripes alternating Amethyst and Yellow, ending with Amethyst.
*Front Shoulder Section:* With 2 strands of Amethyst held together, ch 27. Work same stitch pattern and color stripe as Back Hind Section until 20 rows have been

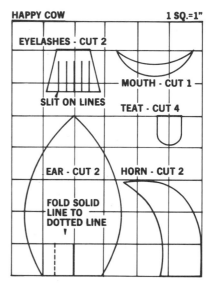

completed—26 sc. *Do not turn at end of last row.* Break off and fasten. *Neck—Next Row:* Attach Amethyst to first sc of last row worked, ch 1, sc in same place, sc in each of the following 13 sc—do not work over remaining 12 sc: change to Yellow in the last sc. Ch 1, turn. *Following Row:* Sc in each sc across. Break off and fasten.
*Back Shoulder Section:* Work same as Front Shoulder Section, working color stripes alternating with Orange and Green.
*Head:* With 2 strands of Pink held together, ch 18. *Row 1:* Sc in 2nd ch from hook and in each ch across—17 sc. Ch 1, turn. *Row 2:* Sc in each sc across. Ch 1, turn. *Row 3:* Make 2 sc in next sc—inc made; sc in each sc across to last sc, inc in last sc—19 sc. Ch 1, turn. *Rows 4-5:* Rpt Rows 2 and 3—21 sc. Work even until piece measures 13½″. *Next Row:* Draw up a loop in first 2 sts, yarn over and draw through 3 loops on hook, dec made; sc in each st across to last 2 sc; dec over last 2 sc—19 sc. Ch 1, turn. *Following Row:* Work even. Ch 1, turn. Rpt last 2 rows once more. *Next Row:* Work even. Break off and fasten. Fold Head in half. Sew 3 edges together, leaving a 2″ opening for stuffing.
*Legs: Inner Leg Section (Make 4):* With 2 strands of Green held together, ch 16. *Row 1:* Sc in 2nd ch from hook and in each ch across. Ch 1, turn. *Rows 2-18:* Work even. Break off and fasten. *Outer Leg (Horizontal Stripe):* Alternating Amethyst and Yellow for stripe pattern, make 1 leg same as inner leg. Now work 1 more leg in same way, using Orange and Green for stripe pattern. *Outer Leg (Ver-*

*Color photo on page 76*

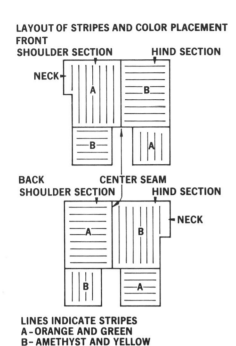

**LAYOUT OF STRIPES AND COLOR PLACEMENT**
**FRONT**
**SHOULDER SECTION**     **HIND SECTION**

NECK

A     B

B     A

**BACK**     **CENTER SEAM**
**SHOULDER SECTION**     **HIND SECTION**

NECK

A     B

B     A

**LINES INDICATE STRIPES**
**A- ORANGE AND GREEN**
**B- AMETHYST AND YELLOW**

*tical Stripe)*: With 2 strands of Amethyst held together, ch 17. Alternating Amethyst and Yellow for stripe pattern, work as for Inner Leg until 17 rows have been completed. Break off and fasten. Make another Outer Leg (Vertical Stripe) alternating Orange and Green stripes.

*Udder:* With Pink starting at lower edge, ch 8. *Row 1:* Sc in 2nd ch from hook and in each ch across—7 sc. Ch 1, turn. *Row 2:* Sc in each sc across. Ch 1, turn. *Row 3:* Sc in each sc, increasing one st at beg and end of row—9 sc. Ch 1, turn. *Rows 4-5:* Work even. Break off and fasten. Make another piece in same way. Sew sides and lower edges of two pieces together.

*Tail:* With Amethyst, ch 22. Work Amethyst and Yellow stripe pattern until 6 rows are completed.

*Mane:* Wind Yellow around a 3″ piece of cardboard 40 times. Double a ½ yd. length of yarn, slip under one end of yarn on cardboard and tie tightly. Slide yarn off cardboard. Cut loops open. Fasten mane to center top of head having half of cut ends coming down over forehead and half falling to back of head.

*Finishing:* Following directions on page 140, enlarge and cut out pattern pieces from felt. Cut mouth of red, eyelashes of black, horns of yellow, teats and ears of pink. Sew mouth, eyelashes and ears in place. Sew two pieces of horn together and stuff. Repeat for other

horn. Sew in place. With black embroidery floss, make two long stitches for nose as shown. Sew teats to udder. Sew each outer leg to an inner leg section on three sides, stuff and sew remaining side. Following chart for layout of stripe and color placement, join pieces as follows: Sew Shoulder and Hind sections of Back and Front together at center seam. Having neck edges together, sew Back to Front, leaving a small opening for stuffing. Stuff and sew opening. Sew legs in place as shown. Sew Udder and Tail in place. Sew head to neck edge.

## LION AND DRAGON PUPPETS
**GENERAL MATERIALS:** White glue; scraps of felt in assorted colors; one 4″×7″ scrap of terrycloth for each puppet, folded in fourths (1¾″×4″). *Note:* See also specific material listings below.

**GENERAL DIRECTIONS:** Following directions on page 140, enlarge patterns for puppets; cut out patterns for body shapes and features. Pin patterns to felt; cut out. Pin front and back pieces together, wrong sides facing; stitch around animals ¼″ from edge, leaving the bottom open where hand operates the puppet. Insert folded terrycloth into

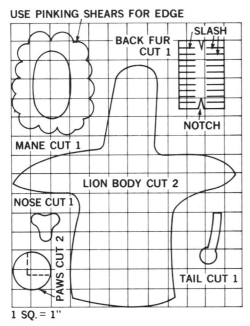

USE PINKING SHEARS FOR EDGE

BACK FUR CUT 1

SLASH

NOTCH

MANE CUT 1

LION BODY CUT 2

NOSE CUT 1

PAWS CUT 2

TAIL CUT 1

1 SQ. = 1"

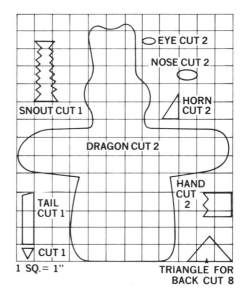

EYE CUT 2

NOSE CUT 2

HORN CUT 2

SNOUT CUT 1

DRAGON CUT 2

TAIL CUT 1

HAND CUT 2

CUT 1

1 SQ. = 1"

TRIANGLE FOR BACK CUT 8

head to give more dimension.

*LION*

MATERIALS: Two 13″ square pieces of felt; 2 beads for eyes (wood, glass or plastic).

DIRECTIONS: Follow general directions for cutting body shapes from 13″ squares of felt and features (fringes, tail, nose and paws) from felt scraps. Glue fringes and tail to front piece, paws to inside of back piece. Cut mane with pinking shears to resemble a daisy without a center. Glue to the front piece. Let

dry, then machine-stitch securely. Sew on eyes. Pin and sew body and stuff lion's head, following general directions.

*DRAGON*

MATERIALS: Two 14″ squares of felt, 2 beads. (glass, wood or plastic).

DIRECTIONS: Follow general directions for cutting front and back body shapes from felt squares and features (eyes, face ridge, nostrils, tail, scales, claws and fangs) from felt scraps. Glue facial features to front of dragon; add scale triangles arranged, overlapping, in order of the spectrum. Glue claws and fangs to inside of back piece; let dry; then stitch securely. Sew beads onto centers of oval felt eyes. Pin and sew body and stuff dragon head, following general directions.

**NUMBER TOSS GAME**

MATERIALS: *For wood base:* 9″ square piece of ½″ pine; ½″-diameter dowel, 8¼″ long; drill with ½″ bit; white glue; tissue paper for patterns; fine grade sandpaper. *For numbers:* Nine pairs of 12″ felt squares, in various colors (2 squares of each color for each number); matching threads; dacron batting.

DIRECTIONS: Following directions on page 140, enlarge and trace patterns onto tissue paper, marking cutout circle for peg. *For each number:* Cut two felt pieces using pattern; cut one piece of batting ⅜″ smaller on all sides than felt number. Pin felt numbers together, with batting in between. Use machine zigzag or close straight stitch to sew all edges closed, including circle for peg. Repeat

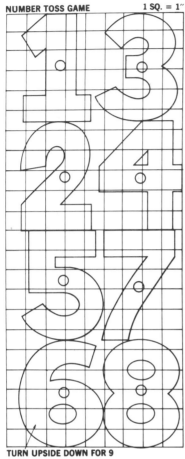

NUMBER TOSS GAME          1 SQ. = 1"

TURN UPSIDE DOWN FOR 9

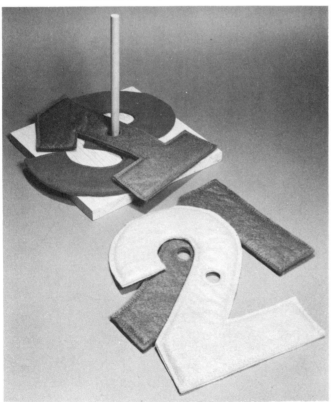

for all numbers. *For base:* Sand any rough edges of 9″ square; drill hole ¼″ deep in center of board. Sand end of dowel; glue dowel into hole.

## TWO-FACED CLOWN PUPPET

Clown puppet is approximately 13″ tall, including cap.

MATERIALS: 4-Ply Synthetic Yarn of knitting worsted weight (4 oz. skeins): 1 skein Yellow (Y), 1 oz. each of white (W), Skipper Blue (B), Orange (O); a few yards of Red (R); crochet hook, size J, *or any size hook which will obtain the stitch gauge below;* small amount of polyester batting for stuffing head; scraps of Black, Red and Light Blue felt.

GAUGE: 7 sc = 2″; 3 rnds = 1″.

*Head:* Starting at center top with W, ch 4. Join with sl st to form ring. *Rnd 1*: 8 sc in ring. Do not join this or any rnd, but mark beg of each rnd. *Rnd 2*: Working in back lp only of each sc, make 2 sc in each sc around—16 sc. *Note:* Work in back lp only of each sc throughout unless otherwise mentioned. *Rnd 3*: * Sc in next sc, 2 sc in next sc; rpt from * around—24 sc. *Rnds 4, 5, 6 and 7*: Sc in each sc around. *Rnd 8*: * Sk next sc, sc in each of next 2 sc; rpt from * around—8 decs made. *Rnd 9*: * Sk next sc, sc in next sc; rpt from * around—8 sc. *Rnd 10*: Sc in each sc around—neck. Cut W.

*Body: Rnds 11-12*: Attach Y; rpt Rnds 2 and 3 of Head. *Rnd 13*: * Sc in each of next 2 sc, 2 sc in next sc; rpt from * around—32 sc. *Rnd 14*: Sc in each sc around. *Rnd 15*: Sc in next sc, ch 4, sk next 4 sc for armhole, sc in each of next 12 sc, ch 4, sk next 4 sc, sc in each of next 11 sc. *Rnd 16*: Sc in each sc and in each ch around—32 sc. Rpt Rnd 14, 15 times. At end of last rnd, sl st in next sc. Cut yarn and fasten.

*Right Sleeve:* Working from wrong side, attach Y to first sc of 4 skipped sc on Rnd 14 (at any side of body) working through both lps of each st, sc in same sc, sc in each of next 3 sc, sc in side edge of next sc on Rnd 15, sc in each of 4 ch, sc in side of next sc—10 sc. Do not join. *Rnds 2, 3 and 4*: Working through both loops of each sc, sc in each sc around. *Rnd 5*: * Ch 1, sc in back lp of next sc; rpt from * around, ending with ch 1, sl st in first ch-1. Cut Y and fasten. *Hand:* Attach W to free lp of first sc on Rnd 4, inside sleeve, working in free lps of sts along Rnd 4 of sleeve, make sc in same st, sc in each of next 9 sts. *Next 3 Rnds*: Working through both lps of each sc, sc in each sc around. *Next Rnd*: (Sk next sc, sc in next sc) 5 times. *Next Rnd*: (Sk next sc, sc in next sc) 2 times; sk next sc. Draw up a lp in each of next 2 sc, yarn over hook, draw through all 3 lps on hook. Cut yarn and fasten. Mark this as right sleeve.

*Left Sleeve:* Using B (instead of Y), work along left armhole, following directions for Right Sleeve; including hand.

*To Stuff Head:* Turn body inside out over head. Stuff head firmly, leaving enough space at center for a finger.

*Inner Section:* With W, ch 10. Join with sl st to form ring. *Rnd 1*: Sc in same ch as joining, sc in each ch around. Do not join. *Next 5 Rnds*: Working through both lps of each sc, sc in each sc around. *Next Rnd*: (Sk next sc, sc in next sc) 5 times. *Next Rnd*: (Sk next sc, sc in next sc) twice; sk next sc, sl st in next sc. Cut yarn and fasten. Insert inner section into center of head; arrange stuffing evenly around crocheted piece, sew starting chain to wrong side of next rnd. Turn body right side out.

*Hair:* Hair is worked in free lps of sc's. Mark 4 sc in line with sleeve on Rnd 8 at each side of head. Attach O to free lp of first sc of marked sts on one side of head, sc in same st, ch 2, working along Rnd 8 make sc and ch 2 in each of next 3 sts; turn, working toward top of head in line with previous sts, along next rnd (Rnd 7 of head), make sc and ch 2 in each of 4 sts, then sc and ch 2 in next st (5 sc in this row); turn, along next rnd make sc and ch 2 in each of 6 sts; turn, along next rnd sc and ch 2 in each of 5 sc, sc in next st. Cut yarn and fasten. Work hair on opposite side of head in same manner. For top of head, attach O to sc in next rnd, above beg of last row of left side hair (above left sleeve), sc in same st, ch 2, sc and ch 2 in each sc around; do not join. Work sc and ch 2 in each sc on next rnd to within last 7 sc (forehead), sc in next sc. Cut yarn and fasten. One side of head has two rows of hair above forehead, other side has only one.

*Hat:* Starting at tip with Y, ch 2. *Rnd 1*: 4 sc in 2nd ch from hook. *Note*: Work in back lp only of each sc throughout. *Rnd 2*: 2 sc in each sc around—8 sc. *Rnd 3*: (Sc in next sc, 2 sc in next sc) 4 times—12 sc. *Rnd 4*: Sc in each sc

around. *Rnd 5*: (Sc in each of next 2 sc, 2 sc in next sc) 4 times. *Rnd 6*: Rpt Rnd 4. *Rnd 7*: (Sc in each of next 3 sc, 2 sc in next sc) 4 times—20 sc. *Rnds 8 and 9*: Sc in each sc around. At end of last rnd, sl st in next sc. Cut yarn and fasten. *Rnd 10*: Attach B to same sc as joining, sc in same st, ch 2, make sc and ch 2 in each sc around. Join to first sc. Cut yarn and fasten. Place hat to top of head and sew securely in place.

*Pompon:* Wind B approximately 30 times around a 1″ square of cardboard. With a separate strand tie at one end; cut at opposite end. Trim evenly. Tack pompon to tip of cap.

*Ruffles:* With basting lines mark center front and center back of body, from neck to lower edge. *First Half*: Attach Y to back lp of first st (after basting) at lower edge of right side half of body (half with Y sleeve), working along lower edge, make sc and ch 2 in back lp of each sc across halfway around to within next basting line; working in free lps of sts (inside basting), make sc and ch 2 in st above on next rnd, continue to work sc and ch 2 up

*Color photo on page 78*

center of body to neck, sc and ch 2 in each st halfway around neck and down center to body to lower edge. Join with sl st to first sc. Cut yarn and fasten. *Second Half*: With B, crochet ruffle along other half of body in same manner.

*Finishing:* Darn in all loose ends on wrong side. *For each face*, from Black felt, cut two ⅜" squares for eyes; from Red felt, cut two ⅜" circles for cheeks and one crescent shaped piece for mouth. *Nose:* With R yarn, ch 2; 4 sc in 2nd ch from hook. Sc in each of 4 sc just made, sl st in next sc. Cut yarn and fasten. Sew or paste features on each face, as shown in photo, placing mouth with corners up on side with two rows of hair above forehead for "happy face"; place mouth with corners down on opposite face for "sad face." Cut a pear shaped piece of Blue felt for tear drop and paste to lower corner of one eye on sad face.

## TWIN STUFFED DOLLS

MATERIALS: ½ yd. (36"- or 45"-wide) peach percale; scrap of nonwoven bondable interfacing; 2-ounce skein four-ply wool or synthetic yarn; one bag polyester stuffing; thread to match fabric and yarn; four flat two-hole buttons, ½" diameter; rug thread and extra large darning needle; scissors; pencil; paper for pattern; pins; embroidery thread scraps and needle; sewing needle; white percale or muslin for lining (optional). *Note:* If fabric of proper color is not available, white cotton can be easily dyed peach or flesh color.)

DIRECTIONS: BODIES: Following directions on page 140, enlarge and cut out all pattern pieces. Pin pieces to fabric and cut out fabric. (*Note:* If you wish a smoother result, cut all pieces again out of thin white cotton and baste to wrong side of each major part of doll. Treat the results as you would the fabric alone.) Sew all darts as indicated. Sew center back seam, leaving opening as indicated. Sew back to front of body. Slash seam allowance as indicated. Turn to right side. Stuff very firmly. This is most important. Pack stuffing until "skin" is almost as firm as that of a composition doll. Sew back opening closed. Sew legs in pairs, leaving bottom of foot open. Slash seams as indicated. Turn to right side. Stuff as firmly as body. Iron sole interfacing and tack. Gather

open end of leg lightly so that it curves under and position sole, facing side inside, over it. Sew sole in place to cover seam (gathering) at opening. Attach legs to body with rug thread on darning needle. The thread is knotted on the outside of a button and pulled as tightly as possible. Gather edge of cover for button and pull to make edge turn under. Sew over button to cover it. Sew arm pieces in pairs. Slash seams as indicated. Turn to right side. Stuff firmly to line and sew across by hand. Turn in top seam allowance and stitch closed. Pin top edge to body at right angle to side seam at shoulder. Sew to body. Cut nose, gather edge, stuff and sew to face. Sew ear pieces in pairs (boy only), leaving opening. Turn to right side, sew opening closed and sew to head. Lightly mark eyes and mouth with pencil and embroider with Satin and Outline Stitches. (*See* BASIC EMBROIDERY STITCHES.)

*To sew hair to dolls:* Using yarn, make hair: *For boy:* fringe around edge of head first, then work down center part. (Sew strands centered on seam.) *For girl:* work with two needles, one working down center part and the other at hairline. (Some loops do not return quite to ear; work to cover scalp.) Add braids when head is covered.

## CLOTHING

MATERIALS: Two pairs of infant size white stretch socks; one square yellow felt (for angel wings); one pair size 9-11 white stretch socks; size 3/0 snaps; fabric remnants (if fabric is to be purchased, ¼ yard is sufficient in almost all garments; floor length garments require ⅓ yard); thread to match all fabrics and trim; paper for patterns; pins; needle; scissors; pencil; (for trim, see individual items).

DIRECTIONS: Following directions on page 140, enlarge and cut out desired patterns.

*Socks:* Cut according to pattern, using finished edge of infant's sock as top of doll sock. Sew. Turn to right side.

*Girl's Panties:* Cut pattern out of white cotton. Leave back opening. Make narrow hem on legs and back opening. Turn in ½" at top and make hem. Sew snap to back. Adjust waist with tiny tucks, if necessary.

*Petticoat:* Cut pattern out of white cotton; sew as indicated. Make rolled hem at neck and arm openings (⅜") and ½" hem at bottom.

Overlap back when edges have been finished (see diagram note). Tack for about ½" up from bottom edge. Sew lace to bottom over hem stitch line. Sew snaps to back.

*Plaid Dress:* Cut fabric according to pattern. Sew diagonal seam of sleeve to diagonal seam of dress front. Repeat to join back. Sew underarm seams. Make dart at shoulder. Turn up ½" on sleeve and make hem. Turn in ½" on back opening and make hem. Bottom edge has ¾" hem. Cut bias of same fabric and bind neck opening. Sew lace to trim sleeves. Finish back as for petticoat.

*Apron:* Cut fabric according to pattern. Make ⅜" hem on all unseamed edges. Sew lace trim as shown. Sew snap to back at neckline.

*Flowered Dress:* Follow directions for plaid dress except make 1" sleeve hems. Sew lace trim to front before binding neck edge.

*Girl's Coat:* Cut material as for dress but use wider pattern for front. Make ½" hems on sleeves and bottom, turn in front edge 1". Sew darts on sleeve. Cut lining in same way and sew into coat but do not sew dart in sleeve top. Neck edge of coat and lining are sewn together but are raw edges. Bind neck with matching bias. Sew snaps to front. Sew tiny buttons to outside of front. *Hood:* Cut 3½"×11" piece from same fabric. Fold in half crosswise and seam to form hood. Cut 2½"×11" piece fur cloth. Seam, right sides together, to front edge. Allow ⅝" for "fur" to show on outside and turn rest to inside of hood. Turn up ½" on neck edge. Cut lining and sew to form hood. Line hood. Sew large white pompon to point of hood on outside. Sew front points (neck edge) of hood to collar at front sleeve seam. Gather back to match neck of coat. Tack at center back.

*Girl's Robe:* Cut fabric according to pattern. Sew in same way as dress. Sew hem as follows: sleeves ¾", front edges ¾", bottom ½". Add lace trim on front before binding neck. Sew snap at neck. Add ribbon bow.

*Nightgown:* Cut piece according to pattern without sleeves. Sew side seams. Bind arm openings. Turn in ½" on back edges and hem. Tack arm openings together at neck and bind neck edge. Make ¾" bottom hem. Sew lace trim. Finish back as for dress.

*Angel—Petticoat:* Follow directions for nightgown, but make narrow hem instead of

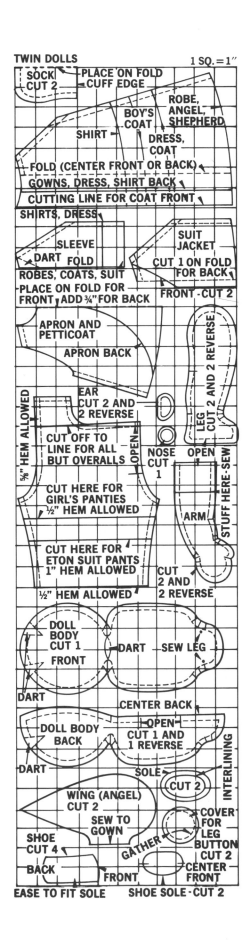

118

*Color photo on page 77*

binding neck and arm openings (tack at shoulders). Use no lace. *Gown:* For sleeve, place pattern ½″ from fold line. Assemble as for dress but use very narrow hem on sleeve and bottom edges. Make no dart at shoulder, gather fullness in tightly. Turn in back edge and finish as for dress. Bind neck. Sew narrow gold rickrack as shown. Cut wings of yellow felt. Sew trim. Sew wings to back of gown by stitching tabs to gown (top of tab begins just below neck bindings). Halo is two 12″ gold pipecleaners twisted together and shaped. Or use wire wrapped with gold tinsel. Shape. Pin to back of head.

*Shepherd:* Cut and make undergown, following directions for angel petticoat. Cut outer robe according to pattern but allow only ¼″ beyond fold line for front opening. Turn in and hem front and sleeve edges ½″. Make 1″ hem at bottom. Bind neck. Crook is pipecleaner. *Head Cloth:* Cut 8½″×9½″ piece thin fabric. Make narrow hem on all edges. Band is ½″ wide black elastic cut 9½″ long and seamed at cut edges.

*Boy's Coat:* Cut fabric to length shown on pattern. Assemble in same way as for girl's coat but omit hood.

*Scarf:* Cut one yard 1″ wide ribbon in half and sew together to make piece 2″ wide × 18″ long. Fringe ends.

*Cap:* Cut off ribbed portion of man's acrylic sock. Gather cut end tightly on wrong side. Turn to right side. Sew large pompon to outside of gathered end. Turn up cuff.

*Mittens:* Make like Socks, but fit to hands.

*Shirt:* Cut fabric to length indicated on pattern. Assemble as for girl's dress except make sleeve hem ⅝″ and turn it up on right side to make cuff. Plaid shirt has "tie" of 3″ square of fabric fringed on all edges and gathered diagonally. Sew to neck edge. White shirt has tiny buttons sewn down center front. Add ribbon bow tie.

*Overalls:* Cut fabric according to pattern. For top edge, sew bias binding but turn it entirely to inside. Make narrow hem at back opening. Cut 2¼″ square pockets and turn in all edges. Sew to overalls. Cut 6″×2″ straps. Fold in half, lengthwise; turn in raw edges and sew closed. Attach to bib. Cross in back and snap to top of back.

*Long Pants:* Cut fabric according to pattern. Make like overalls but without bib and pockets. Turn in top edge ⅝″ and hem. Sew snap to back. Adjust waist with tucks, if necessary.

*Pajamas:* Make bottoms like long pants. Sew top like shirt, but make it ½″ longer and make opening at front.

*Robe:* Cut as for girl's dress. Turn in ½″ on front edges and hem. Turn up sleeves ¾″ hem. Make narrow bottom hem. Bind neck with pajama fabric. Sew snaps to front. Add cord tie.

*Shoes (and slippers):* Cut pieces out of felt according to pattern. Sew front and back seams of tops with tiny overcast stitches. Sew sole to bottom edge (ease if necessary) in same way. Add trim—pompon for slippers, felt bow for girl's dress shoes, cross stitches of embroidery thread for "ties".

*Suit—Jacket:* Cut fabric according to pattern, using same sleeves as for other garments but adjusting sleeve length afterward (bind edge, no hem). Assemble jacket. Bind all edges. Sew soutache just above binding. Sew snaps to front and buttons to outside.

*Pants:* Cut fabric according to pattern. Turn up 1″ and hem bottom edges. Finish otherwise like girl's panties.

# Household Gifts to Make and Give

## CROCHETED OVAL PLACEMAT
*(Placement measures 19"×11")*

MATERIALS: Coats and Clark's O.N.T. Speed-Cro-Sheen Mercerized Cotton: Two balls will make one placemat; steel crochet hook, no. 1/0 (zero).

DIRECTIONS: Starting at center. ch 40 to measure 8". *Rnd 1*: 2 dc in 4th ch from hook, dc in next 35 ch, 6 dc in last ch, working along opposite side of starting chain, dc in each ch across, make 3 dc in same place where first 2 dc were made. Join with sl st to top of starting chain. *Rnd 2*: Ch 3, dc in joining, 2 dc in next dc—*1 dc increased*; inc 1 dc in next dc, dc in next 35 dc across straight edge, inc 1 dc in each of next 6 dc; dc in next 35 dc across other straight edge, inc 1 dc in each of last 3 dc. Join to top of ch-3. *Rnd 3*: Ch 1, sc in joining, (ch 2, sc in next dc) 4 times; (ch 2, skip next dc, sc in next dc) 19 times; (ch 2, sc in next dc) 8 times; (ch 2, skip next dc, sc in next dc) 20 times; (ch 2, sc in next dc) 3 times; ch 2. Join to first sc. *Rnd 4*: Ch 3, (2 dc in next sp, dc in next sc) 4 times; (dc in next sp, dc in next sc) 20 times; (2 dc in next sp, dc in next sc) 8 times; (dc in next sp, dc in next sc) 19 times; (2 dc in next sp, dc in next sc) 3 times; 2 dc in last sp. Join to top of ch-3—126 dc, counting ch 3 as 1 dc. *Rnd 5*: Ch 3, dc in next dc and in each dc around. Join to top of ch-3.

*Rnd 6*: Ch 1, sc in joining, * ch 2, skip next dc, sc in next dc. Repeat from * around, end with ch 2. Join to first sc. *Rnd 7*: Ch 3, (2 dc in next sp, dc in next sc) 5 times; (dc in next sp, dc in next sc) 21 times; (2 dc in next sp, dc in next sc) 10 times; (dc in next sp, dc in next sc) 22 times; (2 dc in next sp, dc in next sc) 4 times; 2 dc in last sp. Join to top of ch-3—146 dc. *Rnds 8–9*: Repeat Rnds 5 and 6. *Rnd 10*: Ch 3, (2 dc in next sp, dc in next sc) 7 times; (dc in next sp, dc in next sc) 22 times; (2 dc in next sp, dc in next sc) 15 times; (dc in next sp, dc in next sc) 21 times; (2 dc in next sp, dc in next sc) 7 times; 2 dc last sp. Join to top of ch-3—174 dc. *Rnds 11–12*: Repeat Rnds 5 and 6. *Rnd 13*: Ch 3, (2 dc in next sp, dc in next sc) 11 times; (dc in next sp, dc in next sc) 21 times; (2 dc in next sp, dc in next sc) 24 times; (dc in next sp, dc in next sc) 20 times; (2 dc in next sp, dc in next sc) 10 times; 2 dc in last sp. Join to top of ch-3. *Rnd 14*: Repeat Rnd 5—220 dc. *Rnd 15*: * Ch 3, holding back on hook last loop of each dc, make 2 dc in sl st, thread over and draw through all 3 loops on hook—*2-dc cluster made;* ch 4, make a 2 dc cluster in 4th ch from hook, skip next 3 dc, sl st in next dc. Repeat from * around, end with skip last 3 dc. Join to base of first cluster. Break off and fasten. Block to measurements.

## ANGEL NAPKIN RING ORNAMENTS

MATERIALS: *For 4 angels:* 1 recipe Basic Salt Dough (see page 7); 5″-diameter plate; cardboard tubes from paper towels or bathroom tissue, cut to 5″ lengths; cardboard; aluminum foil; rolling pin; paper clip; toothpick; nail; paint brush; water; poster or acrylic paints; gold metallic paint; spray varnish or shellac.

DIRECTIONS: Cover cardboard tubes with foil. Roll out a portion of dough to approximately ¼″ thickness. Using a 5″ plate as guide, cut one circle of dough for each 2 angels; cut each in half. Using a partially unbent paper clip, make impressions in the half-circles (for "feathers") in a wing-like pattern. Lay foil-wrapped tubes on a cooky sheet; gently wrap one of the half-circles around each, tucking ends under. Cut rectangular pattern for body from cardboard 1½″ × 3″; round the top slightly for head. Place pattern on another portion of rolled-out dough; cut one body for each angel. Brush body back lightly with water and lay over wings, centering body on wings. Add two small balls of dough for feet, using knife or toothpick to delineate toes. Add two small balls for hands; delineate fingers using knife or toothpick, as shown in photo. Slightly flatten ball of dough for face, using toothpick to poke holes for eyes. Place a ball of dough at top of head; use nail to make center hole so angel can also be used as hanging ornament. Place 2 smaller balls on each side of center, pressing lightly with nail to make a pattern (see photo). If you wish, use toothpick to impress design into body. Gently remove foil-covered tubes. Place in oven preheated to 325° for about 1 hour or until completely hard.

*Note:* If body begins to puff, prick with toothpick and gently press to flatten. Lower oven temperature by 50° and continue to bake. Let cool; paint body with acrylic or poster paints; use gold metallic paint for wings and halo. Face, hands and feet can be left natural. Spray all exposed surfaces with clear varnish or shellac.

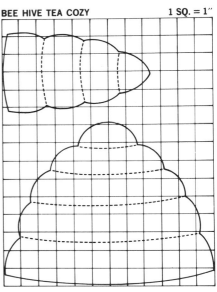

BEE HIVE TEA COZY    1 SQ. = 1″

## BEE HIVE TEA COZY

Fits 23″-diameter pot, 8″ high.

MATERIALS: ½ yard 45″-wide quilted cotton; 1 package black folded bias tape; large spool black thread; spray adhesive; 3 artificial bees and 3 attaching "eye", fasteners, or 3 bee appliqués; straight pins; scissors; paper for pattern; tailor's chalk.

DIRECTIONS: Following directions on page 140, enlarge and trace pattern onto paper. Spray wrong side of fabric; fold to make a doubled piece 18″×22½″. Trace two of each pattern onto fabric. Using a machine straight stitch, stitch over tracing of outside lines. Mark inside horizontal lines with tailor's chalk. Set machine to closest and widest zigzag and stitch across all inside horizontals marked on fabric. Cut out pattern pieces as close as possible to the outside of the straight stitched line. Wrong sides facing, pin and sew sections together over previously straight stitched lines. To make top loop for hanging, sew together a strip of bias tape 2½″ long. Fold tape in half and place it against top point of one wide side of tea cozy with the folded part facing downward and the cut edges on the top center point. Pin and sew down along stitching line of cozy, reinforcing it back and forth. *To bind edges:* Starting at the base of one side section, cover raw edges with bias tape; pin down and sew to top of section. Do the same to opposite section. Then go around the entire piece up to the top. After just passing over the loop, fold loop upwards (so that loop stands up) and stitch back and forth again to reinforce. Continue downward to the base. Starting near a corner of one side section, run bias tape around the entire base, flattening at the corners and overlapping to finish, with the edge of the bias tape tucked in. Sew down 3 eyes and wrap the wire from the artificial bees around eyes. They can be removed for washing. Or, stitch on bee appliqués.

## APPLIQUÉD APPLIANCE COVERS

MATERIALS: Simplicity pattern #5495 for blender, electric mixer and 4-slice toaster; quilted fabric for covers (see pattern for amounts for each cover); Wright's double-fold bias tape (see pattern for amount); 1 yd fusible webbing; zigzag sewing machine; ruler; scissors; straight pins; iron; dressmaker's carbon paper; tracing wheel; paper for tracing; washable cotton and polyester fabrics (except where indicated) and thread.

*For blender:* 5″×9″ pink fabric; 2 pieces 5″×9″ pale blue organdy, voile or any other stiff fabric with transparency; threads: medium blue, fuchsia, royal blue. *For electric mixer:* ½ calico napkin or 6″×12″ calico fabric; 6″×9″

brown fabric; 6″×9″ pink fabric; 3″×3″ vanilla fabric; 2″×2″ red fabric; threads: medium blue, russet, fuchsia, maroon, pale yellow.

*For toaster:* ½ calico napkin or 5″×12″ calico fabric; 5″×8″ russet fabric; 5″×8″ brown fabric; 2″×2″ bright yellow fabric; 3″×4″ pale yellow fabric; threads: medium blue, maroon, pale yellow gold.

*Color photo on page 79*

GENERAL DIRECTIONS: Following directions on page 140, enlarge appliqué pattern and trace onto paper. Lay tracing over corresponding colored sections and trace onto fabric with dressmaker's carbon. Follow Simplicity pattern guide to cut out sections of appliance covers. Following manufacturer's instructions for webbing, fuse appliqué sections together, and then center and apply appliqué to pattern section. After following specific directions below for sewing down the appliqué, return to Simplicity pattern guide to complete construction of cover. For sewing down appliqué, set the length of the stitches very close to give the effect of satin stitching. Stitch width will be indicated (1-4) in the instructions following.

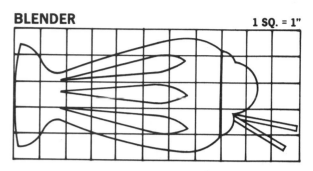

**BLENDER**       1 SQ. = 1″

DIRECTIONS: *Blender:* (*Note:* "Glass" is made up of two layers of fabric. Only one has the cutouts in the center.) Fuse appliqué together by sandwiching the cut-out section between the plain one and the pink. Then fuse down to pattern section. Glue a scrap of fabric on the wrong side for stiffness before stitching straws (stitch width 4). (Backstitch to secure ends.) Then stitch down pink (3) and glass (2½).

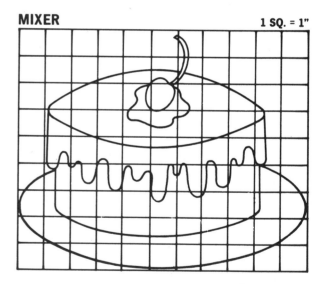

**MIXER**       1 SQ. = 1″

*Electric Mixer:* Fuse together brown, pink and calico sections. Fuse to pattern part and stitch down in this order: plate (3), chocolate cake (3), pink icing (3). Glue white topping and cherry down. Glue a scrap of fabric on the wrong side for stiffness in back of cherry stem. Stitch topping first (2). Stitch around cherry (2½). For stem, start at (1¾) and work up to (4) at the top. (Backstitch to secure ends.) Stem base is stitched (1) at ends, working up to (1½) at center.

*Toaster:* Fuse bread and crust together and down to plate. Fuse to pattern section and sew in this order: plate outside (2¾) and

**TOASTER**    1 SQ. = 1"

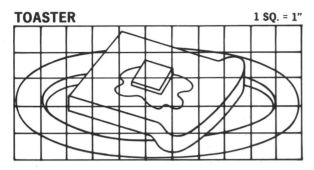

inside, then toast (2½). Fuse down butter. Sew melted butter (2) and pat (outside 2, inside 1½).

## KNITTED POTHOLDERS

MATERIALS: Knitting needles, 1 pair No. 7, or any size needle which will obtain the stitch gauge; rug yarn in your choice of colors (one 4-ounce skein will make about 2½ potholders); fabric in color or print contrasting to the yarn (¼ yard of 45" wide fabric is ample for 5 potholders, or any scrap measuring 8"×8" will make 1 potholder); embroidery needle or any other needle with an eye large enough for the thread; carpet or other heavyduty thread in color coordinated with the yarn and fabric.

GAUGE: 4 sts =1"; 16 rows = 2".

DIRECTIONS: Cast on 27 sts and K56 rows, or until potholder measures a square about 7"×7". Bind off, make a loop with the end of the yarn. This will be used to hang the potholder from a hook. Use the potholder as is, or sew on a fabric square on one side for a decorative effect. To do so, cut an 8-inch square of fabric; turn the edges under to fit the potholder size. Place the fabric on knitted square, turned edges not showing. Baste fabric to square. Then with the needle and a double strand of thread, make a small (⅛") running stitch around the edges of the fabric. Remove basting thread and press. For a second, smaller coordinated potholder, cast on 24 stitches and K48 rows, or until square is about 6"×6".

## HEART-SHAPED POTHOLDERS

MATERIALS (for 2 potholders): ⅓ yd. red corduroy; ¼ yd. red print cotton; ¼ yd. red solid cotton; ⅓ yd. very heavy pellon or padding; two 6" pieces double-fold bias tape; red thread; scissors; pencil; paper for pattern.

DIRECTIONS: Following directions on page 140, enlarge and trace heart designs onto paper; cut out. Cut two hearts size 4 from the pellon or padding. Cut two solid red cotton

**HEARTS**    1 SQ. = 1"

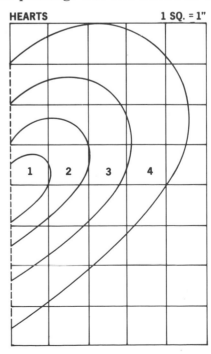

hearts size 2; two print hearts size 3; four corduroy hearts size 4. Appliqué size 2 heart onto size 3 heart. Appliqué this onto a corduroy heart. Place the padding on the wrong side of appliquéd hearts and stitch straight stitches ¼″ from edges. Stitch 6″ piece of double-fold bias tape lengthwise. Fold in half and stitch ends together to form loop. Place loop on right side of top center of corduroy heart, stitched ends up and overhanging ½″. Place appliquéd corduroy heart on top, right side down. Stitch together, ½″ from edges, leaving opening on one side edge for turning. Turn right side out; slipstitch closed. Quilt potholders by stitching one row of straight stitches along the outer edge of the appliquéd hearts.

## NATURAL SPICE RACK

MATERIALS: 1⅛″ lattice: two tops 11¾″ (A), two bottoms 11¾″ (B), four sides 14½″ (C), four shelves 11¾″ (D), four corner pieces 3″ (H); ⅞″ lattice: four fronts 12¼″ (E), four corner pieces 3″ (G); 1⅜″ lattice: four backs 12¼″ (F); ¾″ nails; wood glue; miter box or back saw; hammer; C-clamp; wire cutters or pliers.

DIRECTIONS: (Note: Be careful when nailing so as not to crack the wood.) Cut all pieces using either miter box or back saw. Glue and nail two side pieces (C) to one top piece (A). Repeat with remaining A and C pieces. Glue and nail two side pieces (C) to one bottom piece (B). Repeat. You are now working with two separate units. Glue and nail two back pieces (F), one at top back and one at bottom back of one unit. Glue and nail two front pieces (E), one at top front and one at bottom front of remaining unit. Glue and nail two shelves (D) 4½″ apart, to each unit. Glue and nail remaining front and back pieces (E and F), centered on shelf, to each unit. You are now ready to join the units. Place one unit on its side. Glue one corner piece (G) flush with top and side pieces; clamp. (Note: Before nailing any corner piece, tap nail to start, remove and cut with wire cutters or pliers to ½″ length.) Place second unit parallel to first with same piece G flush with top and side pieces of the second unit. Glue and clamp. Allow glue to dry; nail. Repeat with remaining corner pieces G. You are now working with one unit. Stand unit upright and glue

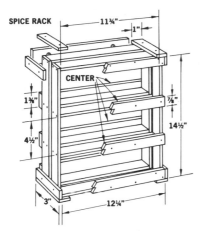

and nail corner piece H flush with front E, back F, and corner pieces G. Repeat with remaining corner pieces H. (*Note:* You can make this spice rack to your own specifications to fit any size spice bottles you might already have.). You are now ready to stain or paint your spice rack, or leave it natural as we did.

## EIGHT-ARM CHANDELIER
MATERIALS: (*Note:* Decorative finials are available in a wide variety of styles and sizes; check the millwork department of your lumberyard. Sizes given are approximate; diameters refer to base.) Eight 2½"-long, 1"-diameter finials; one 5"-long, 1½"-diameter finial; one 1¾"-long, 1½"-diameter finial; eight 2"-diameter flat wood knobs; 5½" of 2×2 lumber; 18" of 1¼" dowel; 5' of 5/16" dowel; white glue; enamel in colors of your choice; polyurethane finish; 1" screw eye; antique chain, length as needed; screw hook.
DIRECTIONS: Cut eight 1½" lengths of 1¼" dowel, and eight 7" lengths of 5/16" dowel. For each candle holder section glue a knob to one end of a 1¼" dowel piece. Drill a ¾" hole through the center of the knob to hold the candle. Drill the other end of the dowel to accommodate a 2½"-long finial; glue on finial. Paint as desired; also paint other finials.

Drill a 5/16"-diameter, ½"-deep blind hole centered ¾" above the bottom of the dowel. Glue a length of 5/16" dowel in the hole. Round the top and bottom corners of the 2×2 with sandpaper. Drill 5/16"-diameter, ½"-deep blind holes in each side of the 2×2, centered ½" from one end. Drill similar holes at the same level in each corner. Drill the end of the 2×2 below these holes as necessary to ac-

commodate the 5" finial; glue in place. Drill other end of 2×2 and glue in 1¾" finial. Glue arms into holes in sides of 2×2. Apply polyurethane finish. Insert screw eye in top finial. Place chain through screw eye. Hang from ceiling hook driven into a joist or beam.

## FOUR-WAY CANDLE STAND
MATERIALS: 14" of 5/4(1 1/16")×6 pine; polyurethane finish.
DIRECTIONS: Cut as shown in diagram. Drill ¾"-diameter, 1"-deep blind holes in top ends of each piece. Apply finish. Fit together as in photo.

**FOUR-WAY CANDLE STAND**

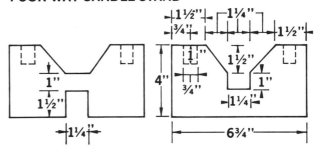

## FINIAL CANDLE HOLDERS
To make the finial candle holders simply drill candle-size holes in the tops, then paint.

*Color photo on page 79*

## ICE CREAM CONE NEEDLEPOINT
MATERIALS: Pencil; sheet of white paper approx. 9½" × 13"; felt-tipped pen; #10 needlepoint canvas; Persian yarn: black, lt. brown, med. brown, raspberry, vanilla, orange, lavender, pink, lt. yellow, lt. orange, lt. pink; masking tape; scissors.

■-Black •-Light Brown ▲-Medium Brown PK-Pink V-Vanilla R-Raspberry O-Orange
LO-Light Orange LY-Light Yellow L-Lavender LP-Light Pink

DIRECTIONS:

1. On large sheet of white paper, enlarge pattern following directions on page 140. Trace over outline with felt-tipped pen.

2. Cut out a piece of needlepoint canvas which is 2″ larger on each side than enlarged pattern.

3. Secure paper pattern to a flat surface with masking tape. Tape needlepoint canvas over the pattern so there is a 2″ border around the picture.

4. Trace the picture onto the canvas using a felt-tipped pen. Remove the canvas and bind the four edges with masking tape.

5. Stitch around all outlines of picture with black yarn, using the Continental Stitch (see BASIC NEEDLEPOINT STITCHES).

6. Using the Continental Stitch throughout, follow color guide given in pattern.

7. When needlepoint is completed, block canvas and press lightly if necessary. Mount needlepoint on a stiff piece of cardboard, taping the unworked 2″ border to the back. Frame as desired.

## LINENS TO TRIM

Elegant "designer" linens are budget-minded Christmas gifts when you become the designer! It's easy to do when you trim solid-colored towels, facecloths, sheets and pillowcases with contrasting braid, rick rack, lace or striped tape. Simply machine-stitch the trims near the borders of the linens, using matching thread. All trims should be washable, of course.

*Color photo on page 79*

## GRANNY TRIANGLE PILLOWS

MATERIALS: *For bottom pillow:* One 4 oz. skein each of 100% wool knitting worsted in the following colors: purple, rose, saffron (yellow), robin blue; two 12"-diameter circles of purple felt; polyester fiberfill; size H crochet hook. *For top pillow:* One 4 oz. skein each of the following colors: dark rust, teal blue, medium rust, cranberry; two 12"-diameter circles of medium blue felt; polyester fiberfill; size H crochet hook.

*Note:* Directions are given for bottom pillow. Follow these directions for top pillow, using colors in order listed above.

DIRECTIONS: *FRONT:* Make 5 Granny triangles for each pillow. *For each triangle:* With robin blue, ch 4, sl st to 1st ch to form. ring. *Rnd 1*: 12 sc in center of ring, sl st to 1st sc. *Rnd 2*: Ch 1, * skip next sc, work a cluster of 5 dc in next sc, skip next sc, repeat from * 2 more times, end off. *Rnd 3*: Attach saffron to back of 3rd dc in any cluster, skip next 2 dc spaces, * make a cluster of 7 dc in next sc space, skip next 2 dc spaces, 1 sc in next dc space, repeat from * 2 more times, end off. *Rnd 4*: Attach rose to back of 4th dc in any cluster, ch 1, 1 sc in same space, ch 2, 2 sc in same space, * 1 sc each in next 7 back spaces, 2 sc in next space, ch 2, 2 sc in same space, repeat from * around, sl st to 1st sc, end off. *Rnd 5*: Work in both top loops, attach purple to any ch 2 corner, ch 3 (counts as 1 dc), 1 dc in same space, ch 2, 2 dc in same space, * 1 dc each in next 11 sc spaces, 2 dc, ch 2, 2 dc in next corner, repeat from * around, sl st to top of 1st dc, end off. *Rnd 6*: Work in top back loop only, attach robin blue in back loop of 1st ch in any corner, ch 1, 1 sc in same space, ch 2, 2 sc in next ch, * 1 sc each in next 15 spaces, 2 sc in ch back, ch 2, 2 sc in next ch back, rpt from * around, sl st to 1st sc, end off. *To assemble 5 triangles:* With robin blue, picking up back loops only whipstitch triangles together.

*BACK:* To make flat round piece for back of pillow, use purple yarn in single crochet, increasing at a gradual but systematic rate to keep the shape flat. Work as follows: Ch 4, sl st to 1st ch to form ring. Make 6 sc in the ring. Make 2 sc in each st around until there is a circle with 12 stitches. It helps if you put a bobby pin as a marker in the last st of each rnd. Then make 2 sc in each st until the circle

has 24 stitches around its edge. Remember to move the marker on each rnd. Now make rnd with only 1 sc in each st, working evenly. Move marker. Next rnd inc in every 2nd st. Next rnd, again work even. The idea is to alternate: first an even rnd, then a rnd inc every second st, another even rnd, then a rnd inc every 3rd st, another even rnd, then a rnd inc every 4th st, and so forth. Continue until your circle is the same diameter as the connected triangles. This will be approximately 20 rnds or 12" in diameter. *Lining:* Sew 2 purple felt pieces together, leaving 3" opening for stuffing. Stuff lightly and evenly with polyester fiberfill. Slipstitch closed. *To assemble:* Place front and back crocheted pieces over felt pillow base, right sides up. With robin blue yarn, whipstitch 2 sides together.

## NEEDLEPOINT PILLOWS

The two top pillows are stitched on 10-hole canvas with 3-strand Persian yarn, using remnants of colors from other needlework projects. A combined total of 4 to 4½ oz. should be more than adequate to complete each pillow. These pattern ideas can be transferred to any size canvas. The bottom pillow in the photo is stitched on 5-hole Penelope canvas with rug-weight yarn.

For beginners, a Half Cross Stitch on Penelope canvas is a practical choice. (*See* BASIC NEEDLEPOINT STITCHES).

*Color photo on page 79*

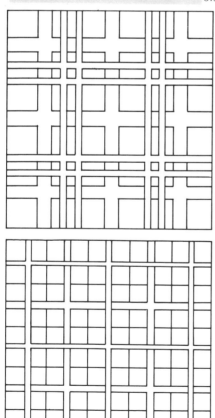

To figure out the quantity of yarn you need, stitch a square inch on the canvas you plan to use and then rip it out and measure the amount (or use 24″ pre-cut strands and keep track of how many you need). When this has been determined, multiply by the size of the finished design in each color.

MATERIALS: One piece of needlepoint canvas at least 16″×16″ (finished size of all three pillows is 14″×14″); masking tape to bind the edges; approximately 4 to 4½ oz. assorted color yarn (be sure to double-check that yarns are colorfast and mothproof); tapestry needle, waterproof felt-tip marker in a neutral color or acrylic paints and brush sold in needlework shops; ½ yard velvet fabric for backing; a piece of brown wrapping paper same size as pattern.

*Transferring the Pattern:*
Place canvas on a flat, even surface. Outline the 14″ area you will be stitching. Draw a vertical and horizontal line marking the center of the canvas. If you use #10 canvas, you will be working with 140 holes in each direction. If you are using #5 canvas, you will be working with 70 holes in each direction.

Then using the photo and the drawings as a guide, transfer the design onto the canvas, dividing up colors and blocks proportionately. Use a ruler and be sure to match up the lines of the pattern with the rows on the canvas. Draw on the stripes first and then fill in the larger squares. When you are satisfied with the arrangement, bind the edges of the canvas with masking tape and you are ready to begin stitching.

*Stitching:*
Work in Half Cross Stitch or Continental

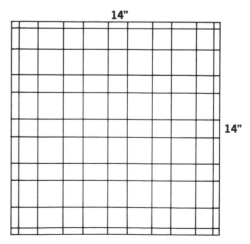

Stitch. (*See* BASIC NEEDLEPOINT STITCHES)

*Blocking:*
Outline the size of the finished pillow square on a piece of brown paper. Place finished needlepoint face down on a flat surface. Using rustproof tacks or pins, tack top and one side in place, spacing tacks about ½" apart and matching up to the outline on the paper. Pull and hold needlepoint piece in taut position and tack remaining sides in place. Moisten the canvas back with water but do not saturate. Let needlepoint dry thoroughly while flat (do not stand upright). If pressing is necessary, cover needlepoint with damp cloth and press on the wrong side with a warm iron.

*Finishing:*
Remove the blocked needlepoint from the board. Machine- or securely hand-stitch all around the needlepoint section of the canvas as close as possible to the worked area without overlapping onto it. Repeat this twice around the entire shape. Cut canvas 1" larger than stitched shape.

To cover a knife-edge pillow, cut the backing fabric to same size as trimmed, blocked canvas. Place right sides of needlepoint and backing together and stitch closed on three sides, using yarn or carpet thread. Trim backing fabric at seams to ⅝". Turn right side out and fill with pillow form or stuffing. Turn open edges under and whipstitch closed. Or, insert a zipper in open edge, following package directions.

## CROCHETED STRIPS AFGHAN
Directions are given for afghan to measure approximately 43"×64", plus 5" fringe.

MATERIALS: Bear Brand Winsom (2 oz. skeins): 6 skeins of Melon Whip (A), 5 skeins of Spearmint (B), 2 skeins Winter White (C); crochet hook, Size H *or any size hook which will obtain the stitch gauge below;* tapestry needle.

GAUGE: 4 sts = 1". Each strip measures 4¾" wide.

*Note:* Leave 6" length at beg and end of each row. Ends can be incorporated with fringe.

FIRST STRIP—*First Half: Row 1 (wrong side):* With A, ch 256 to measure 65"; cut a piece of cardboard 1½" wide and about 3" long; work a loop st in 2nd ch from hook as follows: hold cardboard in back of chain, insert hook in ch st, wind yarn from back to front around the 1½" width of cardboard, yarn over hook and draw through ch st, yarn over hook, draw through the 2 loops on hook—*loop st made:* make a loop st in each ch across—255 loop sts. Break off and fasten.

*Row 2:* With B, make a loop on hook, turn last row with loops up, insert hook from back to front in each of first 3 loops, holding loops tog as 1 unit, make an sc, work 1 more sc through same 3-loop group, * ch 2, insert hook from back to front through each of next 3 loops, holding loops tog, make sc; rpt from * across, ending with ch 2, 2 sc through last 3 loops— 85 (3-loop) groups. Break off and fasten. Turn. *Row 3:* Attach C to first sc on last row, ch 1, sc in same sc, sc in next sc, * ch 2, sc in next sc; rpt from * across, ending with ch 2, sc in each of last 2 sc. Break off and fasten. Turn. *Row 4:* Attach B to first sc, ch 1, sc in same sc and in next sc, * ch 3, sc in next sc; rpt from * across, ending with ch 3, sc in each of last 2 sc. Break off and fasten. *Next Row (opposite edge):* With right side facing, working along opposite side of starting chain, with B, work sc in each ch across. Break off and fasten. Mark this row.

*Second Half of Strip:* Work same as for First Half. *To Join Halves:* With right sides up, place the 2 halves side by side with marked rows tog. With B and tapestry needle, working in back loop only of each sc, from right side sew halves together with an overcast stitch, being careful to work with an even loose tension to keep seam as elastic as crocheted strip.

SECOND STRIP: *omitting Row 4 on Second Half only,* work and sew the 2 halves of strip same as for First Strip.

*To Join Strips:* With right side facing, attach B to first sc on Row 3 of second half of second strip, sc in same st, ch 1, drop loop from hook, pick up first strip and with right side up, insert hook in first sc on Row 4 of any half of first strip, pick up dropped loop and draw through st on hook, ch 2, sc in next sc on second strip, * ch 1, drop loop from hook, insert hook in center ch of next ch-3 on first strip, pick up dropped loop and draw through ch, ch 2, sc in next sc on second strip; rpt from * across to within last sc, ch 1, drop loop from hook, insert hook in last sc on first strip, pick

up dropped loop and draw through sc, ch 2, sc in last sc on second strip. Break off and fasten.

THIRD STRIP: Joining strip being made to free long edge of last strip completed same as second strip was joined to first strip, work same as for Second Strip. Continue to work and join strips same as third strip until a total of 9 strips have been completed.

*Finishing*: Pin afghan to measurements on a padded surface; cover with a damp cloth and allow to dry; do not press.

*Fringe*: Wind A loosely several times around a 5½" square of cardboard; cut on one edge, making 11" strands. Continue to cut strands as needed. Cut B and C strands in same manner. Hold 2 B strands together and fold in half to form a loop; with right side facing, working along ends of rows, insert hook from back to front in end st of a B row and draw loop through, draw loose ends (including end strand of row) through loop and pull tightly to form a knot. Tie two B 11" strands (plus end of row) in same way in end st of each B row; 2 C strands in end st of each C row; tie 3 A groups of 3 strands each evenly spaced along end loop of each A row. Tie fringe along opposite edge in same manner. Trim fringe evenly.

## BED-OF-ROSES AFGHAN

MATERIALS: Bernat Mohair-Plus (1½ oz. sks.): *For Afghan*: 10 sks. of Lt. Pink, 6 sks. Peach and 3 sks. Olive Green; Berella "4" Knitting Worsted, 100% Orlon acrylic, 4 Ply: 3 sks. White. *For Pillow*: Pillow can be made from yarn left over from afghan, *plus* 1 more sk. of Peach Mohair-Plus; ½ yd. lt. pink velvet; 14" pink zipper; 14" form pillow. Crochet Hook, Size G, *or any size hook which will obtain the motif measurement below.*

GAUGE: Each rose motif measures 6" square.

AFGHAN—*Rose Motif A (Make 24)*: With Pink, ch 5. Join with sl st to form ring. *Rnd 1*: Ch 1, (sc in ring, ch 3) 8 times. Join with sl st to first sc—8 ch-3 lps. *Rnd 2*: * In next ch-3 lp make sc, ch 1, hdc, ch 1 and sc; sl st in next sc; rpt from * around—8 petals. *Rnd 3*: Ch 1, working in back of petals, sc around bar of first sc on Rnd 1, * ch 4, sc around bar of next sc on Rnd 1; rpt from * around, end with ch 4. Join with sl st to first sc—8 lps. Break off and fasten. *Rnd 4*: Attach Peach to any sc on last rnd, * in next ch-4 lp make sc, ch 1, (hdc, ch 1) twice and sc; sl st in next sc; rpt from * around, end with sl st in same sc where Peach was attached. *Rnd 5*: Ch 1, working in back of petals, sc around bar of first sc on Rnd 3, *ch 4, sc around bar of next sc on Rnd 3; rpt from * around, end with ch 4. Join to first sc—8 lps. Break off and fasten. *Rnd 6*: Attach Green to any ch-4 lp, sc in same lp, * ch 3, in next lp make 3 dc, ch 2 and 3 dc—*corner*; ch 3, sc in next lp; rpt from * around, end last rpt with ch 3. Join to first sc. Break off and fasten. *Rnd 7*: Attach White to ch-2 sp at any corner, ch 4, in same sp make dc, ch 2, dc, ch 1 and dc; *sk next 2 dc, in next dc make dc, ch 1 and dc; in next sc make tr, ch 1 and tr; in next dc make dc, ch 1 and dc; sk next 2 dc, in corner ch-2 sp make dc, ch 1, dc, ch 2, dc, ch 1, and dc; rpt from * 2 more times; sk 2 dc, in next dc make dc, ch 1 and dc; in next sc make tr, ch 1 and tr; in next dc make dc, ch 1 and dc. Join with sl st to 3rd ch of ch-4. Break off and fasten. *Rnd 8*: Attach Peach to ch-2 sp at any corner, ch 3, in same sp make dc, ch 3 and dc, holding back on hook last loop, dc in same sp, drop Peach, pick up Pink and draw a Pink lp through lps on hook—*color change made*; * place Peach along top edge of last rnd, with Pink, working over Peach, dc in each st and each ch to within last st before next corner ch-2 sp, dc in next dc, changing color to Peach; with Peach, working over Pink, make 2 dc, ch 3 and 2 dc in next corner ch-2 sp, changing to Pink in last dc; rpt from * 2 more times; with Pink dc in each st and in each ch across rem edge. Join to top of ch-3. Break off and fasten. *Rose Motif B* (*Make 24*): Using Peach instead of Pink for Rnds 1, 2 and 3 and Pink instead of Peach for Rnds 4 and 5, work same as for Rose Motif A.

*Finishing*: Alternating motifs A and B in checkerboard fashion, arrange motifs into 8 rows of 6 in each row. With Pink and a darning needle, working through back lp only of each st, sew motifs tog, matching sts and corner sps. When all motifs are joined, tie corners tog as follows: Cut a strand of Peach 20″ long, fold in half and cut on fold. With wrong side of afghan facing, slip Peach double strand through 2 diagonal opposite corner sps in any place where 4 motifs meet. Tie ends into a single knot; turn afghan to right side and bring yarn ends to right side through other 2 opposite corner sps. Tie ends securely into a small bow. Tie corners of each 4-corner group tog in same manner throughout afghan. Along entire outer edge of afghan, tie bows through 2 corner sps (instead of 4 corner sps). There are no bows in the 4 corners of afghan.

*Border*: *Rnd 1*: With right side facing, attach Peach to any corner ch-3 sp; ch 3, in same sp make dc, ch 3 for corner and 2 dc, dc in next Peach dc, dc in next Peach dc, changing to Pink (same as on Rnd 8 of motif), with Pink, working over Peach strand, dc in each of next 15 Pink dc, changing to Peach in last dc; with Peach working over Pink strand, dc in next 2 dc, 2 dc in next sp, sk joining, 2 dc in next sp; *always changing color in last dc of each color group and working over color not in use, continue to make with Peach, dc in each Peach dc and 2 dc in each sp and with Pink dc in each Pink dc across to within next corner sp of afghan; in corner sp with Peach make 2 dc, ch 3 and 2 dc; rpt from * around, ending last rpt with Peach dc in last 2 dc. Join with sl st to

top of ch-3. Break off and fasten. *Rnd 2*: Attach White to any corner ch-3 sp, ch 4, in same sp make dc, ch 3, dc, ch 1 and dc, *ch 1, sk next dc, dc in next dc—*ch-1 sp made*: continue to make ch-1 sps across to within next corner ch-3 sp, ch 1, in corner sp make dc, ch 1, dc, ch 3 for corner, dc, ch 1 and dc; rpt from * 2 more times; make ch-1 sps across rem edge, end with ch 1. Join to 3rd ch of ch-4. Break off and fasten. *Rnd 3*: Attach Peach to any corner ch-3 sp, in same sp make sc, ch 3 and sc; ch 1, * make sc and ch 1 in each ch-1 sp across to next corner sp, in corner sp make sc, ch 3, sc and ch 1; rpt from * 2 more times; sc and ch 1 in each rem sp. Join to first sc. Break off and fasten. *Rnd 4*: Attach Pink to any corner sp, ch 6, dc in same sp, *dc in each sc and in each ch-1 sp across to within next corner ch-3 sp, in corner sp make dc, ch 3 and dc; rpt from * 2 more times; dc in each sc and in each sp to end of rnd. Join to 3rd ch of ch-6. Break off and fasten. *Rnd 5*: Rpt Rnd 2, but do not break off. *Rnd 6*: Ch 3, dc in same st as joining, * sk next dc, in corner sp make 2 dc, ch 3 and 2 dc, sk next dc, make 2 dc in each dc across to within 1 dc before corner sp, rpt from * around, end with 2 dc in each rem dc. Join to top of ch-3, *Rnd 7*: Sl st in each st to next corner sp, sc in corner sp, ch 5, sl st in 3 ch from hook, ch 1—*picot lp made*: sc in same corner sp, *ch 1, sk next 2-dc group, sc in sp between last dc skipped and next 2-dc group, ch 5, sl st in 3rd ch from hook, ch 1, sk 2 dc, sc in next sp between dc's groups; rpt from * around, making sc, picot lp and sc in each corner sp, end with ch 1. Join to first sc. Break off and fasten.

PILLOW TOP: Work same as for Rose Motif A until Rnd 5 has been completed. Break off and fasten. *Rnd 6*: Attach Pink to any sc, *in next ch-4 lp make sc, ch 1, (hdc, ch 1) 3 times and sc; sl st in next sc; rpt from * around, end with sl st in same sc where Pink was attached. *Rnd 7*: Ch 1, working in back of petals, sc around bar of first sc on Rnd 5, *ch 5, sc around bar of next sc on Rnd 5; rpt from * around, end ch 5. Join to first sc—8 lps. Break off and fasten. *Rnd 8*: Attach Peach to any sc *in next lp make sc, ch 1, (hdc, ch 1) 4 times and sc; sl st in next sc; rpt from * around, end with sl st in same sc where Peach was attached. *Rnd 9*: Rpt Rnd 7. Break off and fasten. *Rnd 10*: Attach Green to center of

Color photo
on page 78

any lp, sc in same lp, *ch 3, in next loop make 5 tr, ch 3 for corner and 5 tr; ch 3, sc next lp; rpt from * around, end last rpt with ch 3. Join to first sc. Break off and fasten. *Rnd 11*: Attach White to any corner ch-3 sp, ch 3, in same sp make 2 dc, ch 3 and 3 dc; *sk 2 tr, 3 dc in next tr, sk next tr, dc in next tr, 3 tr in next sc, dc in next tr, sk next tr, 3 dc in next tr, sk 2 tr, in corner sp make 3 dc, ch 3 and 3 dc; rpt from * around, end last rpt with 3 dc in next tr, sk 2 tr. Join with sl st to top of ch-3. *Rnd 12*: Sl st in next 2 dc and in corner sp, ch 3, in same sp make 2 dc, ch 3 and 3 dc; *ch 1, sk 2 dc, dc in next dc, ch 1, sk next dc, dc in next dc, ch 1, (sk next st, make dc, ch 1, and dc in next st) 3 times; (ch 1, sk next st, dc in next st) twice; ch 1, sk 2 dc, in corner sp make 3 dc, ch 3 and 3 dc; rpt from * around, end last rpt with ch 1, sk next 2 dc. Join to top of ch-3. Break off and fasten. *Rnd 13*: Attach Peach to any corner ch-3 sp, ch 3, in same sp make 2 dc, ch 3 and 2 dc; dc in same sp, changing to Pink (same as on Rnd 8 of Afghan motif), * with Pink, working over Peach strand, dc in each dc and in each ch across to next corner sp, changing to Peach in last dc; with Peach, working over Pink, make 3 dc, ch 3 and 3 dc in corner sp, changing to Pink in last dc; rpt from * 2 more times; with Pink dc in each rem dc and in each ch. Join to top of ch-3. Break

off and fasten. *Rnd 14*: Attach White to any corner sp, ch 3, in same sp make 2 dc, ch 3 and 3 dc; *(sk next 2 dc, in next dc make dc, ch 1 and dc) 10 times; in next corner sp make 3 dc, ch 3 and 3 dc; rpt from * 2 more times; (sk next 2 dc, in next dc make dc, ch 1 and dc) 10 times. Join to top of ch-3. Break off and fasten. *Rnd 15*: Attach Peach to any corner sp, *in corner sp make sc, ch 3 and sc; counting each ch as one st make (ch 1, sk next st, sc in next st) 18 times; ch 1; rpt from * around. Join to first sc. Break off and fasten. *Rnd 16*: Work same as Rnd 4 of Afghan Border. Break off and fasten. *Rnd 17*: Attach White to any corner sp, ch 3, in same sp make dc, ch 3, sl st in 3rd ch from hook and 2 dc; *(ch 3, sl st in 3rd ch from hook for picot, sk 2 dc, make 2 dc in next dc) 14 times; ch 3, sl st in 3rd ch from hook, in next corner sp make 2 dc, ch 3, sl st in 3rd ch from hook and 2 dc; rpt from * around, end last rpt with ch 3, sl st in 3rd ch from hook. Join to top of ch-3. Break off and fasten.

*Finishing*: Cut two pieces of velvet each 15″ square. With right sides tog, sew pieces tog along 3 sides, making ½″ seams. Sew zipper in opening. Insert pillow form. Place crocheted pillow top on top of pillow and stitch in place along outer edge, using sewing thread.

# World's Greatest Christmas Goodies

## NOËL PUDDING

*Makes 12 servings.*
- 2 cups all purpose flour
- 1½ cups regular wheat germ (from a 12-ounce jar)
- 2 teaspoons baking soda
- 1 teaspoon salt
- 3 cups fresh or frozen cranberries
- 1 cup dark or light molasses
- ⅔ cup water
- 2 eggs, slightly beaten
  Brandy Glaze (recipe follows)
  Almond slices
  Whole cranberries

1. Combine flour, wheat germ, baking soda and salt in a large bowl; toss in cranberries to coat well. Stir in molasses, water and eggs, just until blended.
2. Spoon into a well-buttered 8-cup tube mold or steam pudding pan; top with steam pudding cover or a double thickness of aluminum foil and tie with kitchen string.
3. Place mold on a rack in a large kettle. Fill kettle with boiling water to half the height of mold; cover kettle.
4. Steam over low heat 2 hours, or until a cake tester inserted near center of pudding comes out clean. Cool in pan on wire rack 10 minutes; unmold onto serving plate; spoon **BRANDY SAUCE** over and garnish with almond slices and fresh cranberries.

COOK'S TIP: Mold can be made well ahead of time; cool completely on wire rack; wrap in heavy-duty aluminum foil and freeze. Remove from freezer the day before serving. To serve warm, place foil-covered pudding in slow oven (300°) 20 minutes or until heated through.

BRANDY SAUCE: Makes about ½ cup. Combine 1½ cups 10X (confectioners' powdered) sugar, 2 tablespoons brandy and a dash of salt in a small bowl. Beat until smooth and creamy.

## HOLIDAY SPRITZ
*Bake at 350° for 12 minutes.*
*Makes 7 dozen.*
 1 cup (2 sticks) butter or margarine
 ¾ cup sugar
 2 eggs
 1 teaspoon vanilla
3½ cups all purpose flour
 ½ teaspoon salt
 ¼ teaspoon peppermint extract
 ¼ teaspoon spearmint extract
  Red and Green food coloring
  Ornamental Frosting (recipe follows)
  Cinnamon red-hot candies

1. Beat butter or margarine with sugar until fluffy in a large bowl with electric mixer at high speed; beat in eggs and vanilla. Stir in flour and salt to make a soft dough.
2. Divide dough between two small bowls. Flavor one bowl with peppermint extract and tint pale pink with a few drops red food coloring. Flavor and tint second bowl of dough with spearmint extract and green food coloring.
3. Fit a snowflake or star plate or disk on an electric food gun or manual cookie-press. Fill with one part of dough at a time and press out onto ungreased cookie sheets.
4. Bake in moderate oven (350°) 12 minutes, or until cookies are firm. Remove from cookie sheet with spatula; cool completely on wire racks. Decorate with swirls of ORNAMENTAL FROSTING through a fancy tube in a pastry bag and top with cinnamon red-hot candies, if you wish.

*Suggested Variations:* For CHOCOLATE SPRITZ: Substitute ¼ cup dry cocoa powder (not a mix) for ¼ cup of the flour and increase vanilla to 2 teaspoons in above recipe; omit other food coloring and flavoring. For COFFEE SPICE SPRITZ: Add 2 tablespoons instant coffee powder and ½ teaspoon ground cinnamon to above recipe and omit other flavoring and food coloring. For BRANDY SPRITZ: Add 1 teaspoon brandy extract and increase vanilla extract to 2 teaspoons in above recipe and omit other flavoring and food coloring. For LEMON SPRITZ: Add 2 teaspoons lemon extract and 2 teaspoons grated lemon rind; omit flavorings and colors.

## BUTTERY CUT-OUT COOKIES
*Bake at 350° for 8 minutes.*
*Makes 3 dozen cookies.*
 ¾ cup (1½ sticks) butter or margarine
1¼ cups sugar
 1 egg
 1 teaspoon vanilla
 1 teaspoon almond extract
2½ cups all purpose flour
 ½ teaspoon salt
  Red food coloring
  Ornamental Frosting (recipe follows)

1. Beat butter or margarine with sugar until fluffy in large bowl with electric mixer at high speed; beat in egg, vanilla and almond extract.
2. Stir in flour and salt to make a stiff dough; tint pink with red food coloring. Wrap in wax paper; chill 3 hours, or until firm enough to roll out.
3. Roll out dough, one quarter at a time, to a ¼-inch thickness on a lightly floured pastry cloth or board. Cut with 3-inch heart-shaped cookie cutter. Place, 1 inch apart, on ungreased cookie sheet. Brush some with a mixture of red food coloring and almond extract, if you wish.
4. Bake in moderate oven (350°) 8 minutes, or until cookies are firm. Remove from cookie sheet with spatula; cool completely on wire racks, then decorate with ORNAMENTAL FROSTING, using tips on a decorating set.

BAKER'S TIP: You can omit the red food coloring and substitute 1 teaspoon lemon extract for the almond extract in this recipe to make a basic cutout cookie.

*Suggested Variation:* For BROWN SUGAR COOKIES, substitute 1¼ cups firmly packed brown sugar for the granulated sugar and 1 teaspoon rum extract for the almond extract.

*Color photo on page 80*

## ORNAMENTAL FROSTING

*Makes about ¾ cup.*

1 egg white
Dash cream of tartar
1¾ cup 10X (confectioners' powdered) sugar
¼ teaspoon vanilla

Beat egg white and cream of tartar until foamy in a small bowl with electric mixer at high speed; lower speed; beat in 10X sugar until frosting stands in firm peaks and is stiff enough to hold a sharp line when cut through with a knife. Keep bowl of frosting covered with damp paper towels to prevent drying.

## THUMBPRINT COOKIES

*Bake at 350° for 10 minutes.*
*Makes 4 dozen.*

1 cup (2 sticks) butter or margarine
¼ cup granulated sugar
¼ cup firmly packed light brown sugar
2 eggs, separated
1 teaspoon vanilla
1 teaspoon rum extract
2 cups all purpose flour
½ teaspoon salt
1 cup finely chopped walnuts or pecans
Candied red and green cherries, halved

1. Beat butter or margarine with granulated and brown sugars until fluffy in a large bowl with electric mixer at high speed; beat in egg yolks, vanilla and rum extract. Stir in flour and salt to make a soft dough.
2. Beat egg whites slightly with a fork in a pie plate. Spread chopped nuts on wax paper.
3. Shape dough, a little at a time, into 1-inch balls; roll first in egg white and then in nuts. Place, 2 inches apart, on a greased cookie sheet.
4. Bake in moderate oven (350°) 5 minutes; remove cookie sheet from oven; make a hollow in center of each ball with a thimble or the back of a wooden spoon. Bake 5 minutes longer, or until lightly browned.
5. Remove cookies from cookie sheets with spatula; cool on wire racks. Fill center of each cookie with halved red or green candied cherries. Store in a tight metal tin.
BAKER'S TIP: You can substitute strawberry or mint jelly or a few semi-sweet chocolate pieces for cherries in the recipe.

## GERMAN STOLLEN

*Bake at 350° for 35 minutes.*
*Makes 2 large loaves.*

1 cup seedless raisins
1 jar (8 ounces) mixed chopped candied fruits
¼ cup orange juice
¾ cup milk
½ cup sugar
1 teaspoon salt
1 cup (2 sticks) butter or margarine
2 envelopes active dry yeast
¼ cup very warm water
2 eggs, beaten
1 teaspoon grated lemon rind
5 cups all purpose flour
1 cup chopped blanched almonds
¼ teaspoon ground nutmeg
2 tablespoons cinnamon-sugar

1. Combine raisins, candied fruits and orange juice in a small bowl.
2. Heat milk with sugar, salt and ½ cup of the butter or margarine; cool to lukewarm. Sprinkle yeast and 1 teaspoon sugar into very warm water in a large bowl. ("Very warm" water should feel comfortably warm when dropped on wrist.) Stir until yeast dissolves; allow to stand until mixture bubbles, about 10 minutes; then stir in cooled milk mixture, eggs and lemon rind.
3. Beat in 2 cups of the flour until smooth; stir in fruit mixture, almonds and nutmeg, then beat in just enough of remaining 3 cups flour to make a stiff dough. Knead 5 minutes, or until smooth and elastic on a lightly-floured pastry cloth or board, adding only

enough flour to keep dough from sticking.

4. Place in a greased large bowl; turn to coat with shortening; cover with a clean towel. Let rise in a warm place, away from draft, 2 hours, or until dough is double in bulk.

5. Punch dough down; knead a few times; divide in half. Roll each into an oval, 15×9; place on a greased large cookie sheet. Melt remaining ½ cup butter or margarine in a small saucepan; brush part over each oval; sprinkle with cinnamon-sugar; fold in half, lengthwise. Cover; let rise again 1 hour, or until double in bulk. Brush again with part of the remaining melted butter or margarine, just before baking.

6. Bake in moderate oven (350°) 35 minutes, or until golden and loaves give a hollow sound when tapped. While hot, brush with remaining melted butter; cool on wire racks.

7. Wrap in heavy-duty aluminum foil; label, date and freeze.

8. To serve, remove foil, place on cookie sheet. Heat in moderate oven (350°) 20 minutes. Sprinkle with 10X sugar, if you wish.

## ARKANSAS JALAPENA CORNBREAD
*Bake at 400° for 35 minutes.*
*Makes three 9-inch rounds.*
  2 packages (8 ounces each) corn muffin mix
  2 cups milk
  ½ cup vegetable oil
  3 eggs, beaten
  1 large onion, grated

  2 tablespoons sugar
  1 can (8 ounces) cream-style corn
  ½ cup seeded and chopped Jalapena (hot green) peppers
1½ cups shredded Cheddar cheese (6 ounces)
  ¼ cup chopped and drained pimiento

1. Combine corn muffin mix, milk, vegetable oil, eggs, onion, sugar, cream-style corn, Jalapena peppers, Cheddar cheese and pimiento in a large bowl; mix just until blended with a wooden spoon.

2. Divide batter among 3 greased 9-inch layer-cake pans.

3. Bake in hot oven (400°) 35 minutes, or until breads are golden. Cool in pans 5 minutes; invert onto wire racks, then turn topside up immediately. Cool completely. Place in plastic bags and seal. Freeze.

## RICH "ALMOST WHITE" BREAD
*Bake at 400° for 30 minutes.*
*Makes 2 loaves.*
  1 cup milk
  1 tablespoon granulated sugar
  1 tablespoon brown sugar
  1 tablespoon molasses
  2 teaspoons salt
  2 tablespoons lard or vegetable shortening
  2 envelopes active dry yeast
  ½ cup very warm water
  2 eggs
  5 cups all purpose flour
  1 cup whole wheat flour

1. Heat milk, sugars, molasses, salt and lard or shortening in a small saucepan; remove from heat; cool to lukewarm.

2. Sprinkle yeast over very warm water in a large bowl. ("Very warm" water should feel comfortably warm when dropped on wrist.) Stir until yeast dissolves.

3. Stir in cooled milk mixture, eggs and 2¾ cups of the flour. Beat with electric mixer at medium speed for 2 minutes.

4. Work in remaining all purpose and whole-wheat flours a little at a time, first with a wooden spoon, then with hands, until dough leaves side of bowl.

5. Turn dough out onto a lightly floured board; invert bowl on dough and let rest 10 minutes. Knead dough 10 minutes, or until smooth and elastic.

6. Round up dough in a ball and put into a

greased large bowl; turn over in bowl; cover with plastic wrap. Allow to rise in a warm place, away from draft, 1 to 1½ hours, or until double in bulk. Punch dough down; cover; let rise 30 minutes.

7. Divide dough in half and knead each piece a few times. Roll out each piece to an 18×9-inch rectangle on board. Roll up, from short side, jelly-roll fashion. Press ends with hands to seal; fold under; place, seam-side down, in a 9×5×3-inch greased loaf pan. Repeat.

8. Cover pans and let rise in a warm place, 45 minutes, or until dough rounds in pan.

9. Bake in hot oven (400°) 30 minutes, or until loaf is golden and gives a hollow sound when tapped.

10. Turn out onto wire racks to cool. When cool, wrap in plastic bags and freeze.

BAKER'S TIP: Should loaves get too dark while baking, place a sheet of aluminum foil over top of bread for rest of baking.

## SWEDISH BEER RYE
*Bake at 350° for 40 minutes.*
*Makes 2 large loaves.*
   2 envelopes active dry yeast
   ¼ cup very warm water
 1¾ cups beer
   ½ cup dark molasses, warmed
   ⅓ cup melted butter or margarine
   1 tablespoon caraway seeds, crushed
   2 teaspoons salt
   3 cups whole-rye flour
   2 cups all purpose flour
   1 cup whole-wheat flour

1. Sprinkle yeast over very warm water in a large bowl. ("Very warm" water should feel comfortably warm when dropped on wrist.) Stir until yeast dissolves.

2. Stir in beer, molasses, butter or margarine, caraway seeds and salt. Beat in rye, all purpose and whole-wheat flours to make a soft dough. Brush surface of dough with melted butter; cover bowl with plastic wrap. Allow to rise in a warm place, away from draft, 1 hour, or until double in bulk; punch dough down.

3. Turn dough onto lightly floured pastry cloth or board; knead 8 minutes, or until smooth and elastic. Divide dough in half; roll to a 13×9-inch rectangle. Roll up tightly from long side, jelly-roll fashion; pinch long seam

tightly to seal. Roll loaf gently back and forth to taper ends. Place loaves on a large cookie sheet which has been greased, then sprinkled with cornmeal; cover with a clean towel.

4. Let rise again in a warm place, away from draft, 45 minutes, or until double in bulk.

5. Bake in moderate oven (350°) 40 minutes, or until bread gives a hollow sound when tapped. Remove from cookie sheet to wire racks; cool completely. When cool, wrap in plastic bags and freeze until gift-giving time.

## UNCLE DAN'S PICKLES
*Makes 6 one-pint jars.*
   7 large cucumbers, sliced
   6 medium-size white onions, sliced
 2½ large sweet red peppers, halved, seeded and chopped
   ¼ cup kosher salt
     Cracked ice or ice cubes
 2½ cups white vinegar
 2½ cups sugar
   1 tablespoon mustard seed
   1 teaspoon celery seed
   ¾ teaspoon turmeric
   ½ teaspoon ground cloves

1. Layer cucumber, onion and pepper slices with salt in a large glass or ceramic bowl; cover with cracked ice or ice cubes.

2. Weight down pickles by placing a plate, just a little smaller than bowl, over ice cubes and stack several large cans on top. Let stand 4 hours. Pour off liquid.

3. Bring vinegar, sugar, mustard and celery seeds, turmeric and cloves to boiling in a large kettle; add drained vegetables and return to boiling. Ladle into hot jars, leaving ½-inch headroom. Seal and process 15 minutes in water-bath, following manufacturer's directions.

4. Store in a cool, dry place at least 1 month.

## PETER PIPER PICKLES
*Makes 6 one-pint jars.*
   8 cups thinly sliced cucumber
   8 large onions, thinly sliced
   2 large sweet red peppers, halved and sliced into strips
   ½ cup salt
   4 cups firmly packed brown sugar
   3 cups cider vinegar
   1 cup water
  12 whole cloves

Color photo
on page 80

*L. to R.: Juarez Tomato Peppers, Wade's Pickles, Chili Sauce, Uncle Dan's Pickles, Pickled Onions, Garden Relish and Peter Piper Pickles. Breads. L. to R.: Swedish Beer Rye, Rich "Almost White" Bread and Arkansas Jalapena Cornbread.*

1 tablespoon turmeric
1 tablespoon mustard seed
1 teaspoon ground cinnamon

1. Layer cucumber and onion slices and pepper strips with salt in a large glass or ceramic bowl. Let stand at room temperature 3 hours. Drain off all liquid from vegetables.
2. Bring sugar, cider vinegar, water, cloves, turmeric, mustard seed and cinnamon to boiling in a large kettle; add drained vegetables; return to boiling.
3. Ladle into jars, leaving ½-inch headroom. Seal and process 15 minutes in water-bath, following manufacturer's directions.
4. Store in cool, dry place at least 1 month.

### GARDEN RELISH
*Makes 8 one-pint jars.*
5½ cups chopped sweet green pepper
2½ cups chopped sweet red pepper
2½ cups chopped cucumber
2½ cups chopped onion
 2 cups chopped celery
1½ cups chopped carrot
 ½ cup chopped hot red pepper
 2 cups granulated sugar
 1 cup firmly packed brown sugar
⅔ cup salt

1 tablespoon mustard seed
1 tablespoon celery seed
1 tablespoon turmeric
3 cups cider vinegar

1. Combine sweet red and green peppers, cucumber, onion, celery, carrot and hot pepper in a very large kettle. Stir in granulated and brown sugars, salt, mustard and celery seeds, turmeric and vinegar with a large wooden spoon until evenly blended.
2. Bring to boiling, stirring several times; allow to boil 5 minutes; remove from heat.
3. Ladle into hot one-pint jars, leaving ½-inch headroom. Seal and process 15 minutes in hot-water bath, following manufacturer's directions.
4. Store at least 1 month in a cool, dark place to develop flavors. Give relish in antique jars, or in jars wrapped with bright gingham, tied at top with a ribbon bow.

### PICKLED ONIONS
*Makes 6 one-pint jars.*
 36 small white onions (about 3 pounds)
 2 tablespoons kosher salt
    Water
 3 cups white vinegar
¾ cup sugar

½ teaspoon whole cloves
6 small whole red Mexican peppers (about
   1½ inches long)
   OR: 6 dried chili pepper pods
6 small bay leaves

1. Soak onions in 1 tablespoon salt and water to cover for 2 hours; peel onions. Soak peeled onions in remaining 1 tablespoon salt and water to cover in a large glass or ceramic bowl 48 hours at room temperature; drain.
2. Bring vinegar, sugar and cloves tied in cheesecloth to boiling in a large kettle; add onions; return to boiling; cook 3 to 5 minutes; remove spice bag.
3. Ladle into hot one-pint jars, leaving ½-inch headroom. Add a pepper and a bay leaf to each jar. Seal and process 15 minutes in water-bath, following manufacturer's directions.
4. Store in cool, dry place at least 6 weeks to develop flavors.

**WADE'S PICKLES**
*Makes 5 one-pint jars.*
16 pickling cucumbers, cut into
   ¼-inch slices (about 4 pounds)
4 cups cider vinegar
3 tablespoons salt
1 tablespoon mustard seed
6 cups sugar
⅓ cups white vinegar
2¼ teaspoons celery seed
1 teaspoon whole allspice

1. Combine cucumbers, cider vinegar, salt, mustard seed and ¼ cup of the sugar in a large kettle. Bring to boiling; lower heat; cover kettle; simmer 10 minutes; drain and discard liquid. Pack into hot pint jars.
2. Combine remaining 5¾ cups sugar, white vinegar, celery seed and allspice in a large saucepan; bring to boiling; pour over cucumber slices, leaving ¼-inch headroom.
3. Seal and process 15 minutes in water-bath, following manufacturer's directions.
4. Store in cool, dry place at least 1 month.

**CHILI SAUCE**
*Makes 6 one-pint jars.*
16 large tomatoes, peeled, cored
   and chopped (16 cups)
2 cups chopped onion
2 cups chopped sweet red pepper

3 hot red peppers, chopped
3 cups white vinegar
1 cup firmly packed brown sugar
2 tablespoons salt
1 teaspoon ground ginger
1 teaspoon ground nutmeg
1 teaspoon ground allspice
2 tablespoons crushed stick cinnamon
1 tablespoon mustard seed
1 tablespoon celery seed
1 teaspoon whole cloves
1 bay leaf

1. Combine tomatoes, onion, sweet and hot peppers, vinegar, sugar, salt, ginger, nutmeg and allspice in a large kettle. Tie stick cinnamon, celery and mustard seeds, cloves and bay leaf in cheesecloth; add to kettle.
2. Bring to boiling; lower heat; cook, stirring several times with a long wooden spoon, 2 hours, or until thick; remove spice bag.
3. Ladle into hot one-pint jars, leaving ½-inch headroom. Seal and process 15 minutes in water-bath, following manufacturer's directions.
4. Store in cool, dry place at least 3 weeks.

**JUAREZ TOMATO/PEPPERS**
*Makes 4 one-pint jars.*
12 small green tomatoes (about 2 pounds)
12 red cherry peppers (about 2 pounds)
2 heads dill
   OR: 2 teaspoons dill seed
4 small cloves garlic
4 small dabs horseradish (about ¼ teaspoon for each jar)
2 teaspoons mustard seed (½ teaspoon for
   each jar)
2 teaspoons mixed pickling spices (½ teaspoon for each jar)
4 cups water
2 cups white vinegar
2 teaspoons salt

1. Wash green tomatoes and cherry peppers well; drain on paper towels. Pack tightly into hot one-pint jars; divide dill, garlic, horseradish, mustard seed and pickling spices.
2. Bring water, vinegar and salt to boiling in a large saucepan; ladle into jars, leaving ½-inch headroom. Seal and process 15 minutes in water-bath, following manufacturer's directions.
3. Store in a cool, dry place at least 1 month.

# How —To

## HOW TO ENLARGE AND REDUCE DESIGNS

When enlarging or reducing designs, it is important that the design stay in proportion. Either of these two methods can be used:

METHOD 1

Make a tracing of the design if it is not already marked off in squares. Depending on the size, now mark off with squares. Use ⅛″ squares for small designs, ¼″, ½″, 1″ squares etc., for larger designs. After you have decided on the size of the enlargement or reduction, mark off on tracing paper the same number of squares, similarly placed, in the area to be occupied by the design. For example, if you wish to make your design four times as large, make each square four times as large. Now copy the outline from your tracing onto the new squares, square by square.

METHOD 2

Make a tracing of the original design. Put an outline around the tracing. Now, as in the diagram, draw a second outline of the final size (this outline will be below and next to the first, corners touching). The new outline is made by drawing a diagonal line through the original, continuing it down through one corner as shown, thus being able to perfectly proportion the new size. Now draw the second diagonal line through both outlines. At the point where the two diagonal lines meet at the center draw one horizontal and one vertical line (you now have four equal areas in each outline). In each of these, complete the other diagonals and then divide further into equal rectangles with additional horizontal and vertical lines. As in Method 1, copy the design from the original, tracing it onto the new outline triangle by triangle. To transfer

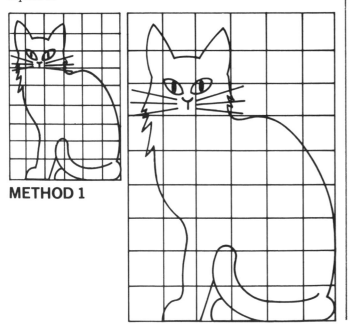

**METHOD 1**

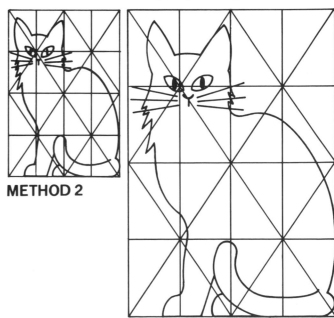

**METHOD 2**

design onto material to be decorated slip dressmaker's carbon between tracing and surface. Trace carefully with pencil. An easy way to divide the rectangle into the spaces described above is to fold a paper the desired size of the design into halves, quarters, sixteenths, etc. Other shortcuts: (1) place a wire screen over the original design for squaring-off; (2) transfer the original design to graph paper . . . clear acetate if available.

Another way to enlarge a design is with Printing Technology Institute's "Craft Plan,"™ a light, transparent, 100% nylon fabric with a printed grid of dots, 1" apart.

## KNIT AND CROCHET ABBREVIATIONS

**beg**—begin, beginning; **bet**—between; **bl**—block; **cc**—contrasting color; **ch**—chain; **dc**—double crochet; **dec(s)**—decrease(s); **dp**—double-pointed; **dtr**—double treble crochet; **gr**—gram; **hdc**—half double crochet; **in(s)** or *"*—inch(es); **incl**—including; **inc**—increase; **k**—knit; **lp(s)**—loop(s); **lp st**—loop stitch; **mc**—main color; **oz(s)**—ounce(s); **p**—purl; **pat(s)**—pattern(s); **pc**—picot; **psso**—pass slip stitch over; **rem**—remaining; **rnd(s)**—round(s); **rpt**—repeat; **sc**—single crochet; **sk(s)**—skein(s); **sk**—skip; **sl**—slip; **sl st**—slip stitch; **sp(s)**—space(s); **st(s)**—stitch(es); **st st**—stockinette stitch; **tog**—together; **tr**—triple crochet; **tr tr**—treble treble crochet; **work even**—work without inc or dec; **yo**—yarn over; **yd(s)**—yard(s); *\**—repeat whatever follows the * as many times as specified; **( )**—do what is in parentheses the number of times indicated.

## BASIC EMBROIDERY STITCHES

### Back Stitch

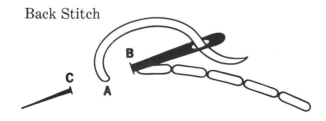

### Blanket or Buttonhole Stitch

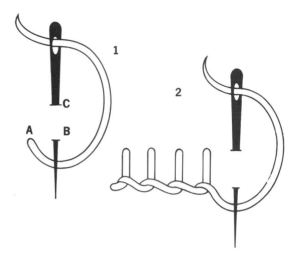

### Chain Stitch

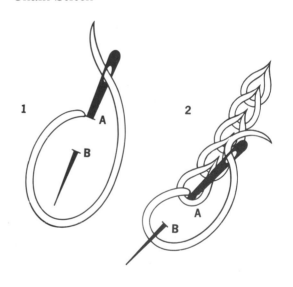

### Closed Buttonhole Stitch

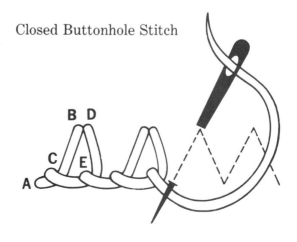

## Couching

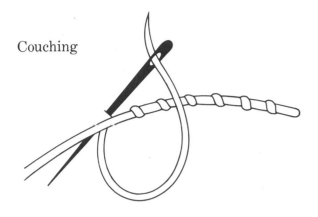

## Fly Stitch

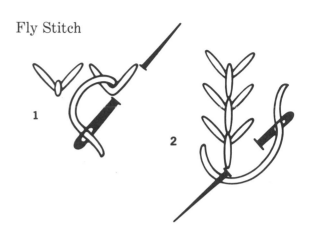

## Cross Stitch

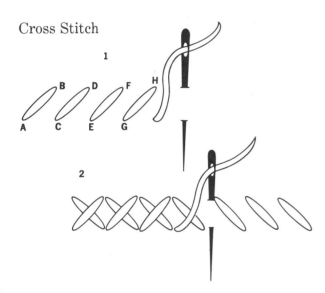

## French Knots

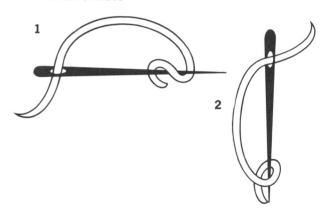

## Duplicate Stitch

## Herringbone Stitch

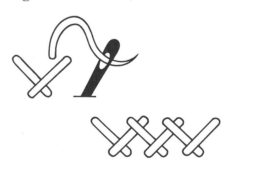

## Feather Stitch

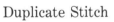

## Detached Chain or Lazy Daisy Stitch

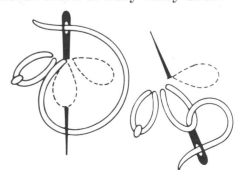

## Long and Short Stitch

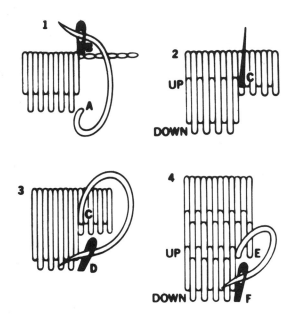

## Outline or Stem Stitch

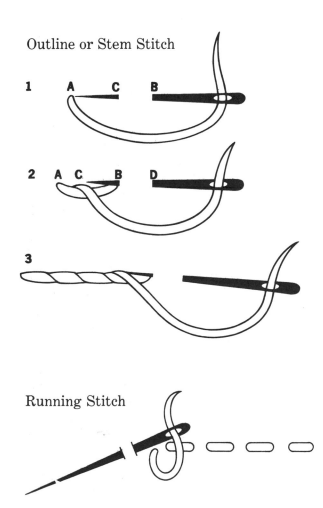

## Running Stitch

## Satin Stitch

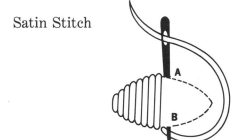

## Split Stitch

## Straight Stitch

## BASIC NEEDLEPOINT STITCHES

### Bargello or Florentine Stitch

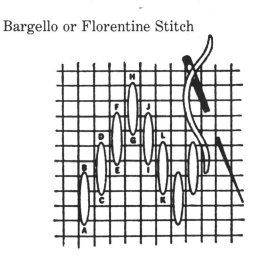

## Basket Weave

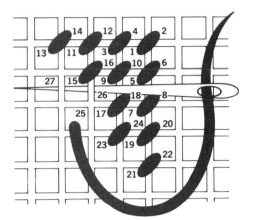

## Cross Stitch

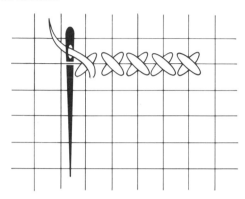

## Chevron Stitch

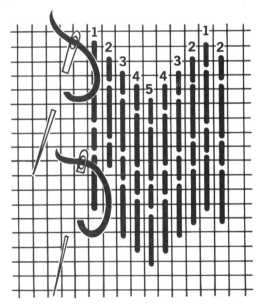

## Half Cross Stitch

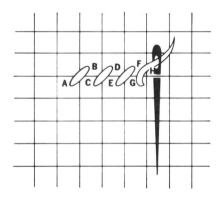

## Continental or Tent Stitch

## Parisian Stitch

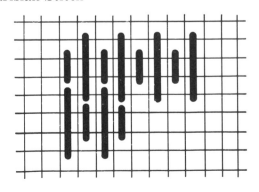